Charles Stephens

DA TIMOTHY CODE

Shepherding the Flock without Fleecing the Sheep

MBOKODO PUBLISHERS

MAKING YOUR DREAM COME TRUE

ISBN 978-1-990919-44-2 (Paperback)

www.mbokodopublishers.eshop.co.za

mbokodopublishers@gmail.com

First Published (2021)

Mbokodo Publishers

P. O. Box 3663

White River

1240

Contents

1. Preamble 9

The Distinction between an Apostle and a Disciple . 9

Bishops, Deacons, Prophets, Pastors, Teacher and Healers 10

Da Timothy Code 10

Methodology 11

2. East Africa 15

The Falasha 15

Ethiopia has a long-standing association with the Queen of Sheba. The thing is that when she came to Jerusalem to meet Solomon, around 1000 BC, she was coming from a Jewish colony in "Sabaea" roughly where Yemen is today. 15

The Nubian Eunuch 16

Prestor John? 16

Frumentius 18

The Rise of Islam 19

The Mountains of the Moon 19

The Martyrs of Uganda 21

St Josephine Bakhita 22

Archbishop Luwum 23

Kenya's Richest Pastors 23

Simony 25

3. North Africa 29

The Holy Family 29

St Mark 29

Africans in the church of Antioch 30

The Scillitan Martyrs 30

Pope Victor I 31

Perpetua and Felicitas 31

Naming Africa 32

Clement of Alexandria 34

Tertullian 35

Chaeremon and Ischyrion 36

Origen 36

Cyprian 37

Maximilian of Numidia 38

Mennas 38

Peter of Alexandria 39

Pachomius the Great 40

Athanasius versus Arius 40

St Augustine 42

Cyril of Alexandria 43

Deogratias 43

Shenoute 44

The Rise of Islam 44

The Way Forward 45

4. **West Africa** **47**

Circumventing Islam 47

Uninhabited Islands 48

The Atlantic Slave Trade 50

Joao Pinto 51

Baltazar Barreira 52

Indigenous Missionaries 53

Dual Citizens 53

Reverend Thomas Thompson 54

The Cost of Discipleship 55

Benson Idahosa 58

Bishop David Oyedepo 58

Enoch Adeboye 59

Chris Oyakhilome 59

T B Joshua 60

Matthew Ashimolowo 60

Lazarus Muoka 61

Chris Okotie 61

Cohabitating with Islam 62

5. Central Africa **64**

From Desert to Jungle 64

Bakongo outreach 66

Mbemba Nzinga 68

Outreach into Angola 68

Mussa Alebik 69

The Mwene Mutapa 70

David Livingstone 72

The Comber family 74

Heli Chatelain 75

Dr Walter Strangway 76

Uebert Angel 81

Prophet Shepherd Bushiri 82

Isaiah Brian Sovi 84

Apostle Miz Mzwakhe Tancredi 84

The Price of Discipleship 85

6. Southern Africa **87**

Krotoa 87

The Hottentot Code 94

George Schmidt 96

Johannes Vanderkemp 97

Ntsikana 100

The Black Circuit 101

Moffat.. 103

Jager Afrikaner... 105

Dr John Philip 106

Tiyo Soga 107

Reformed Church Missionaries 111

Subversive Subservience....................................... 113

Rev. Theophelus Hingashikuka Hamutubangela .. 114

Trevor Huddleson.. 115

Archbishop Emeritus Desmond Tutu.................... 116

Andries Tetane 118

Ray McCauley... 120

Timothy Omotoso 121

7.   **Epilogue** **123**

Re-thinking the criteria for sainthood? 123

Prophets or Profits?.. 123

Paradigm Lost 125

8.   **Recommended Reading**................................ **128**

1. Preamble

The Distinction between an Apostle and a Disciple

There is some overlap in the way these two terms are used, and thus some ambiguity. The simplest way to understand "apostle" is that this core of cadres was trained by Jesus himself. They knew him as a contemporary – the author and finisher of our faith.

Whereas discipling is a function, just like preaching or prophesying. You don't have to be born in the first century to be a disciple. You can join the movement in any century and become a disciple. This is almost synonymous with the term "follower" or "adherent". But it is a bit stronger than the term "believer", it takes some involvement or commitment to be a disciple.

Yet people speak of both the "twelve apostles" and the "twelve disciples" without making any distinction. Perhaps because the term "apostle" came to be used much less, after the first generation of Christianity. Whereas "discipling" continued on unabated. Curiously, however, we still run into church leaders who call themselves "apostles" – twenty centuries later. Perhaps this is to say something spiritual about them?

Bishops, Deacons, Prophets, Pastors, Teacher and Healers

These functions sometimes involve spiritual gifting – like prophecy and faith-healing. Or relevant skills may be acquired like administration and accounting for Deacons. Sometimes the spiritual gifting may be mixed with technical expertise – like teaching.

One teaching method is coaching. Another is mentoring. Paul started as Timothy's coach and eventually changed his mode to mentorship. As a mentor to Timothy, he wrote down what can be regarded as a "baseline" for Christian leadership...

Da Timothy Code

I Timothy chapter 3: *"Here is a trustworthy saying: Whoever aspires to be an overseer desires a noble task. [2] Now the overseer is to be above reproach, faithful to his wife, temperate, self-controlled, respectable, hospitable, able to teach, [3] not given to drunkenness, not violent but gentle, not quarrelsome, not a lover of money. [4] He must manage his own family well and see that his children obey him, and he must do so in a manner worthy of full respect. [5] (If anyone does not know how to manage his own family, how can he take care of God's church?) [6] He must not be a recent convert, or he may become conceited and fall under the same judgment as the devil. [7] He must also have a good reputation with outsiders, so that he will not fall into disgrace and into the devil's trap.*

8 In the same way, deacons are to be worthy of respect, sincere, not indulging in much wine, and not pursuing dishonest gain. 9 They must keep hold of the deep truths of the faith with a clear conscience. 10 They must first be tested; and then if there is nothing against them, let them serve as deacons.

11 In the same way, the women are to be worthy of respect, not malicious talkers but temperate and trustworthy in everything.

12 A deacon must be faithful to his wife and must manage his children and his household well. 13 Those who have served well gain an excellent standing and great assurance in their faith in Christ Jesus."

Methodology

This book is divided into chapters on East Africa, North Africa, West Africa, Central Africa and South Africa. Within each chapter, the timeline moves from the oldest profile to the most recent. For the most part, then, the book moves forward through the centuries.

The continent of Africa has many rivers, but five great rivers define it. The Nile has two tributaries, the Blue Nile out of East Africa and the White Nile from the "great lakes" of central Africa. It runs north through a swamp called the Sudd (hence the name Sudan) that is larger than England. Then its waters reconvene and it flows into Egypt, emptying at the delta into the Mediterranean Sea. The Niger river rises in West Africa and flows east then south, emptying at the delta into the Atlantic Ocean. The Congo river rises deep in

11

central Africa and loops north then west into the Atlantic Ocean. The Zambezi river also rises in central Africa and flows south then east to the Indian Ocean. Finally the Orange river rises in the highlands south of Lesotho and flows right across the continent to the Atlantic ocean. Halfway across the continent, it is joined by the Vaal river, flowing down from the high veld to the north-east. So it seems fitting to adopt a structure of five regions to relate five very different narratives - in the same order that the five rivers are introduced above.

This sequencing allows the author to tell the story of church history in a unique way. It is very impressionistic – moving from one biographical sketch to another through time. So it has a strong human-interest dimension, while rolling out the narrative of each region. It is composed of a series of thought-bursts, like beads on a string.

The book is by no means comprehensive, one could easily fill a whole book on each of these five zones! In fact, many books have been written about single individuals like St Augustine or David Livingstone, who get a page at the most herein! These profiles were cherry-picked in order to show a flow or sequencing. But the story is not told as a narrative – it is told in a series of vignettes. But there is a trending, that is consistent throughout – until very recent decades.

Tertullian said that "the blood of martyrs is the seed of the church". The icons in this book – most of them just short biographical sketches – mostly fall into different phases of persecution or extremely difficult working conditions. However, not all African church leaders suffered or were martyred. Some rose to the top. For example, the first African Pope (Victor I) started under a Roman emperor (Septimus) who was also African. But soon after Victor I died, the Cae-sar Septimus started another period of persecution.

Some African rulers welcomed the arrival of Christianity, others resisted it. The ebb and flow of this inter-action can be followed like a thread through the biographical sketches. The regional stories are very different. For example, Christianity and even Judaism arrived early on in East Africa, but relatively much later in South Africa. So it is better to tell the story in five regional clusters, than as a continental narrative. Also, Christian expansion in North Africa happened during the Roman Empire, whereas the arrival of Christianity in South Africa only came during the Age of Discovery, many centuries later. Once again this fits the regional approach better.

The book is not just history – it raises theological issues that bedevil the 21st century. Throughout all the biographical sketches there is a message – *who moved the goalposts*?

All through the ages, there have been raging debates like the great debate between Arius and Athanasius – both Africans. Our era is no exception. And among the key issues that we are debating today is *Da Timothy Code*. Why can church leaders now be ambitious for money? And if that is not the case, what does it say about those who are so inclined?

A few dates are sprinkled in – to keep the timeline consistent these are most frequently the dates that church leaders died.

One map in each chapter has been inserted too – at the appropriate moment in the running timeline.

2. East Africa

The Falasha

Ethiopia has a long-standing association with the Queen of Sheba. The thing is that when she came to Jerusalem to meet Solomon, around 1000 BC, she was coming from a Jewish colony in "Sabaea" roughly where Yemen is today.

Then around 600 BC, the Sabaeans in turn colonized Africa – across the Red Sea from their Jewish enclave on the Arabian Peninsula. They brought with them their semitic language and script, from which Ge'ez evolved. Amharic is thus a Ethio-semitic language. So the cherished Ethiopian legend that Solomon and the Queen of Sheba had a princely child – Menelik – is rooted in history. Ethiopia's religion was Judaism; its capital was Aksum.

The Falasha are black Jews, descended from this immigration from Sabaea or Sheba. They still worship in Agaw, an ancient Cushite language, although their every-day speech is in Amharic. In recent decades they have been accepted by Israel as authentic Jews.

Ethiopians have often been confused with Nubians. Just as many people still do not make a clear distinction between Nilotics and Bantus as two distinct races – which they are.

The Nubian Eunuch

Christianity arrived very early in both Egypt (North Africa) and Ethiopia (East Africa). To be exact, the encounter in Acts chapter 8 between the apostle Philip and "*an important official in charge of all the treasury of the Kandake*" was not with an Ethiopian official - but with a Nubian. For the civilization of Meroe flourished in the upper Nile region from 300 BC to 300 AD. Its queen was the "Candace", so her chancellor of the exchequer had travelled a very long way to worship at the temple in Jerusalem. He was from a place not far from the confluence of the White Nile and the Blue Nile.

The Nubian church, the Ethiopian church, and the Coptic church in Egypt have close links with the rest of Eastern Orthodoxy, including the churches of Syria and Armenia. It is thought that to escape post-Chalcedon persecutions, many missionaries came to Africa from Syria (i.e. Antioch and Edessa). (This includes the Syrian missionaries of the fifth century, whom Ethiopians remember as the Nine Saints.)

Some observers think that this Syrian influence was behind the stone-hewn churches of Lalibela – built just after 1200 AD.

Prestor John?

This legend is about a Christian king who got cut off and isolated by the rise of Islam. It was one of the drivers of the

Crusades – to free Prestor John. Although there are other possibilities in Asia, the root of this legend could be the Nubian church?

By the fourth century, the kingdom of Aksum was expanding and it conquered Meroe. However, the two cultures are distinct. Even for geographical reasons, Nubian Christianity grew in isolation. The Arabs did not conquer Nubia like they did Egypt, downstream. Like Ethiopia, Nubia was literate using its own script. It was a vibrant culture in its own right.

Gradually, though, Christianity was diminished by a process of erosion – that is, of constant Arab Muslim immigration. The Christian kingdom splintered into smaller kingdoms like Dotawo and Alwa that survived into the fifteenth century. But by the time that a Jewish traveller, David Reubeni, visited the capital Soba in 1523, it lay in ruins.

About this same time, Portuguese vessels were exploring their way around Africa – looking for an alternate route to the Orient. When Vasco de Gama reached the Malabar coast of India in 1498, he said that he had come in search of Christians and spices. Opening the sea-route to Asia would enable the Portuguese to bypass the Muslim middlemen who now controlled the routes through the Near East. In code-language, he was looking for Prestor John. Finding the Christian potentate cut off from the main cluster of Christendom was another quest, not unlike finding the Holy Grail.

This legend survived long after Ethiopia was "rediscovered". For example, in the 1620s, a Jesuit missionary working amongst the Chichewa people in Nyasaland on the Zambezi River was optimistic about finding him north-east of Lake

Malawi. That was 150 years after Bartholemeu Dias circum-vented Africa, but over 200 years before David Livingstone!

Frumentius

One story illustrates how Christian witness can arise through our work, as opposed to conventional missionary outreach. In the fourth century, Frumentius was returning from India to his home town, Tyre, with his boss Meropius (a Christian philosopher) and another friend. During a provisioning stop-over on the Red Sea coast, at the port of Adulis, his boss was killed, and he and his friend Aedesius were seized and en-slaved, in Abyssinia. He was sent to Aksum, where he later became King Ella Amida's private secretary. Aedesius be-came the king's cup bearer. Being good Christians, they worked hard and were faithful to the king.

Frumentius would have seen the stelae and obelisks at Ak-sum, which were erected by King Ezana a century earlier. While at Aksum, he and Aedesius planted a church there.

After years of service in Aksum, the king died and gave the two men their freedom. Aedesius returned home to Tyre. But Frumentius travelled to Alexandria to request a pastor for his church. Patriarch Athanasius, upon hearing his testimony, deemed Frumentius himself to be the most suitable person, and ordained him a bishop! He returned, and eventually many were converted. The Bible was later translated into the Ge'ez language.

In Ethiopia, he is called "Abba Salama" – father of peace. This is a vivid illustration, that when believers apply their beliefs to their work with diligence, some who observe them will perceive the truth with an inner eye of faith. But not everyone.

He died around 360 AD.

The Rise of Islam

This game-changer did not affect East Africa as suddenly or thoroughly as North Africa. In fact, the king of Aksum gave sanctuary to some of the very first Muslims, after they fled from the hostile city of Mecca. Muslim traders gradually settled along the Red Sea and Indian Ocean coasts, but relations with Christians were generally cordial.

Although the Atlantic Slave Trade is much better known, it cannot go unmentioned that Africa was a source of slaves for Arabia and the Middle East. For example, there was a slave market in Zanzibar – an island off the Tanzanian coast that was colonized by Arabs. The lingua franca of east Africa is Swahili – a kind of creole that mixes Arabic with indigenous languages.

The Mountains of the Moon

It goes without saying that Africans who lived on the continent knew its geography long before Europeans did. And just like the Roman Empire only occupied a rim of North Africa, European exploration came mostly by sea – around Africa's perimeter. First down its west coast, then to central Africa, then down to the Cape. And eventually, right around the continent to Arabia and India.

During this period, maps of Africa were romanticized. The perimeter was mapped first but what lay inland was unknown – to Europeans. Missionaries and explorers like the Jesuits and later David Livingstone began to penetrate, looking for the source of the Nile, Prestor John, and Solomon's gold mines. One 1805 map of Africa by Cary illustrates how little Europeans knew, even though at the time it was drawn up to show (ostensibly) how much they knew!

The fact is that there is a mountain range on the border of Uganda and Congo called Rwenzori. Yes, the waters that rise there feed the lakes that flow into the White Nile. These are commonly called the "mountains of the moon" because they are snow-capped all year round, although straddling the equator. The mountain range is north-to-south, not east-to-west as in Cary's map. It is relatively short, not a long line as Cary imagined in his map.

The errors of this map are allegorical. They remind us that maps are not always accurate, even when they look official.

By following them, we can sometimes lose our way instead of finding our way. But they do often contain a kernel of truth, albeit distorted.

The Martyrs of Uganda

These are the 19th century Uganda martyrs who were persecuted by King Mwanga II. In 1885, he first killed an Anglican missionary - bishop James Hannington - and his companions.

Then, when his steward - 25-year old Joseph Musaka Balikuddembe - confronted him about this atrocity, he was burned alive. Musaka was not only the chief steward of Mwanga's court, but also leader of a small community of 200 Christians.

The king appointed Karoli (Charles) Lwanga to take over the instruction and leadership of the Christian community at court, but a third wave of his rage erupted, six months later in 1886 AD. Lwanga and thirty-one other young Christians were burned to death at Namugongo.

RIP: Bishop James Hannington, Joseph Musaka Balikuddembe, Karoli Lwanga, Dennis Sebuggwago, Matthias Kalemba, et alius

"A Christian who gives his life for God is not afraid to die."
(Joseph Musaka)

St Josephine Bakhita

Born a slave in 1869, she was kidnapped by Arab slave traders in Sudan in the late nineteenth century. This was long after the Slavery Abolition Act Bill of 1833 in the UK, and the Proclamation of Emancipation in 1863 in the USA. The scourge of slavery may still be practiced up to the present in a clandestine way, in pockets of Africa, the Persian Gulf, and Asia – in spite of the strong human rights ethos of our time.

Forcibly converted to Islam, she was treated so badly that she forgot her own name. Bought and sold by multiple cruel owners, she later adopted the nickname Bakhita ("Lucky") when she was bought by a relatively kind master, an Italian diplomat who took her home with his family to be their nanny. When he bought a hotel on the Red Sea, he went to live there with his wife while he sent his daughter and her servant Bakhita to stay with Canossian nuns in Venice.

Bakhita officially converted at Easter that year and was baptized "Josephine". When the parents came back, she did not want to leave (especially since she'd be just another slave back in Africa), and the diplomat's wife tried to force her. The mother superior was shocked at this treatment, since Italian law didn't believe in slavery, and called in the authorities to ensure Bakhita's continuing freedom. So she became a Canossian nun herself, and as doorkeeper to the convent in Schio, became beloved by the townspeople for her gentleness, calm voice, and smile.

Her mother superior ordered her to dictate her life story, and it was published in 1930 to great acclaim in Italy. As soon as she died in 1947, people began to call for her canonization. She has been officially named the patron saint of Sudan.

"If I were to meet those slave raiders who abducted me, and the ones who'd tortured me, I'd kneel down to kiss their hands — because without them, I'd never have become a Christian and a woman of faith."

Archbishop Luwum

Janani Luwum was a leading voice in criticising the excesses of the Idi Amin regime that assumed power in 1971. In 1977, Archbishop Luwum delivered a note of protest to dictator Idi Amin against the policies of arbitrary killings and unexplained disappearances. Shortly afterwards the archbishop and other leading churchmen were accused of treason and brutally executed.

He is recognized as a martyr by the Anglican Church and his death is commemorated on the 17th of February every year. His statue is among the Twentieth Century Martyrs at the front of Westminster Abbey in London.

Kenya's Richest Pastors

In recent decades, there seems to have been a sea-change. For example, Wambui Mbuthia wrote an article in The Standard about "Kenya's top eight richest pastors and their net worth". From that article:

"Following the rise of self-established houses of worship, many pastors have derived material wealth and have made it to the top cream of the society.

"Although Kenyans do not have the privilege to know how much such pastors make, it is easy to estimate from the lives

lived by their families, the posh cars they drive around and the estates they move into."

The article goes on to profile eight church leaders admired for their wealth:

- Prophet David Owuor
- Bishop Allan and Rev Kathy Kiuna
- Rev Teresia Wairimu
- Bishop Margaret Wanjiru
- Pastor Thomas Wahome
- Pastor Victor Kanyari
- Bishop Mark Kariuki
- Brother Kamlesh Pattni

We live in an era when African leaders - including church leaders - are being exposed as never before. Legends like the mountains of the moon and Prestor John have given way to a Free Press. What has changed from the narrative of Bakhita and Luwum? *Da Timothy Code* says explicitly that church leaders should not be ambitious for money.

The way of the cross is self-sacrifice. It is not to be listed by the media among the richest pastors in your country; that is not biblical success. That is a distortion of theological standards. To crave wealth is natural to humans. It is supernatural to deny yourself and pastor a flock selflessly. This is a "beautiful attitude" or Beatitude. According to Matthew chapter 5 verses 10 and 11:

"Blessed are those who are persecuted because of righteousness,
for theirs is the kingdom of heaven.

[11] *"Blessed are you when people insult you, persecute you and falsely say all kinds of evil against you because of me. [12] Rejoice and be glad, because great is your reward in heaven, for in the same way they persecuted the prophets who were before you."*

Our map of leadership is inaccurate. It is distorted. It is leading us astray. But those who abide in this Faith know it intimately. It is their home, their natural habitat.

The most reliable map that exists for Christian leaders is I Timothy chapter 3. Tongue in cheek, we call it *Da Timothy Code*. Africa needs to rediscover it.

Leonard Ravenhill put it this way:

"The church right now has more fashion than passion

Is more pathetic than prophetic

And more superficial than supernatural."

Simony

Simon Magus was intrigued when he saw the miracles performed by the apostles. He wanted that same power, to integrate into his magic show. God punished him for that twisted ambition. This is known as "simony".

As it came to be understood in the Catholic church of medieval times, "simony" referred to the purchase of an ecclesiastical office. This was a major problem already at the turn of the millennium. In 1049, a reform movement took root in Rome. To stop "simony", they also had to prohibit "lay investiture". This essentially means that rich lay people (i.e. not trained as, or employed in, the clergy) could not buy

25

their way into church leadership. Controlling the pathway into ecclesiastical office – for example, of becoming a bishop – had to come from a genuine track-record in church leadership.

This papal reform often quoted John 10: 1 – 18 as the point of reference. Christ is the only door to the sheepfold. This was strong imagery. Pope Gregory defined the canonical concepts for "simony" in a way that was flexible. It caused some of his successors to be deposed – like Pope Gregory VI (in 1046)! Scandals presided over by his successor Gregory VII started to refer to "simony" as a heresy. For reformers in the 11th century, this was a serious issue. But some accepted it fatalistically. It was a bit like the controversy of corruption and patronage in our 21st century. Some want to eliminate it, and others see it as "the African way".

Good governance may make it possible for pastors and churches to handle large volumes of wealth – with integrity. But it raises concerns in church circles – about motives. In Luke 16, Jesus said that you cannot serve God and Mammon. Some translations misrepresent this as "God and money". That is not what Jesus said. He said "Mammon" – the Syrian deity of riches. The point is: *"You shall have no other gods before me"*.

"Mammon" became a pejorative term for greed, gluttony, excessive wealth, and unjust enrichment. But Jesus was referring to a familiar deity, implying a warning against church leaders who are (in Paul's terminology) "ambitious for money".

In times of old, lesser gods used graven images or idols as their mask – to interface with worshippers. The next phase was to use a new kind of fronting – human faces like NE-BUchadnezzar and BELchazzar (Nebu and Bel were gods from the Babylonian pantheon). These days they have a new kind of mask – ideologies. When we engage with Humanism (humans at the centre instead of God at the centre), Relativism or Marxism (a secular religion in its own right), we should remember this. So it is with money. It is a material thing that seems innocuous. But there is a god of money behind it called Mammon, who is much more sinister.

This is the logic of St Paul's teaching in *Da Timothy Code* – that you cannot be a church leader and also "ambitious for money". That is a contradiction.

3. North Africa

The Holy Family

The story of the flight into Egypt is a reminder that Jesus himself was a "man of sorrows, and acquainted with grief". He was neither rich nor powerful. He and his parents lived as political refugees in Africa, until the tyrant at home died and they could return.

He died ignominiously on the cross around 30 AD, and rose triumphantly after three days in the grave.

St Mark

John Mark was a native of North Africa (Cyrenaica in the Pentapolis). He has a Jewish name (John) and a Roman name (Mark). So we hazard a guess that his father was Roman, knowing as we do that his mother Mary (sister of the apostle Barnabas) was Jewish. He was coached and mentored by both Paul of Tarsus and Peter bar Jona. In the apostolic comity agreement, John Mark was sent to Egypt. He became the first bishop of Alexandria. This city was the intellectual centre of the Greek world. Mark was martyred there around 70 AD. He is now the patron saint of the Coptic church.

Africans in the church of Antioch

Simon of Cyrene (in North Africa) was no stranger to Jesus when Roman soldiers coopted him to carry the cross. For he was one of the Seventy whom Jesus had trained and sent out on practicums. His sons Rufus and Alexander also became church leaders.

"Simeon called the black" and Lucius were among the founders of the church at Antioch. Very possibly this "Simeon" is the same one who carried the cross to Calvary, for Jesus? We can't be sure of that, but we can be sure of one thing - there was a strong African contingent in the early church, largely because North Africa was very much part of the Roman world.

The Scillitan Martyrs

Twelve African Christians were executed for their beliefs in 180 AD. The Acts of the Scillitan Martyrs are possibly the oldest written records belonging to the African church. This was during the last wave of persecutions under the emperor Marcus Aurelius. It was in Scilli, a town in the Roman province of Numidia.

RIP: Speratus, Nartzalus, Cintinus, Veturius, Felix, Aquilinus, Laetantius, Januaria, Generosa, Vestia, Donata, and Secunda.

According to the correspondence of St Augustine, there was another incident around the same time at another location. These were the Madurian martyrs, led by Namphamo, who Augustine considered to be Africa's protomartyr. None of these Christians would recant.

Pope Victor I

In Arabic, "Al Maghrib" means "west". The sun rose in the "Levant" and set in "Al Maghrib". The rim of North Africa in the western Mediterranean was colonized by the Phoenicians (i.e. Lebanese) long before the rise of Rome as the super-power of the whole Mediterranean world. The Atlas mountains are a special feature of this region. Its major city was Carthage, and its lingua-franca was Phoenician, not Greek as in the eastern Mediterranean region. Especially under Hannibal, Carthage was a fierce opponent of Roman domination.

A Berber from this region called Victor rose to the post of Pope in Rome from 189 AD until his death in 199 AD. He was the first African Pope. It was under Victor I that Latin replaced Greek as the official language of the Western church. Victor I was the first Pope to have direct dealings with the imperial court in Rome. So there were periods of détente as well as of persecution during this era.

Perpetua and Felicitas

Only one year after Iranaeus bishop of Lyons was martyred in 202 AD, came the torture and execution of these two courageous African ladies in Carthage. A 22-year noble woman Vivia Perpetua and a pregnant slave girl Felicitas were martyred together under the persecution of Septimus. That Roman emperor was also an African. He was born in Leptis Magna (present day Al-Khums, Libya) in the Roman province of *Africa*.

RIP: Secundulus, Saturninus, Saturus, and another slave Revocatus, who were martyred with them. They told the judges, "You judge us now, but God will judge you". They would not recant.

Rarely have women been venerated by so many, for so long! In Carthage, a magnificent basilica was afterwards erected over the tomb of these two women martyrs, the Basilica Maiorum, where an ancient inscription bearing their names has been found. Saints Felicitas and Perpetua are two of seven women commemorated by name in the second part of the Canon of the Mass.

The once-flowering rambling rose "Félicité et Perpétue" (R. sempervirens x 'Old Blush') with palest pinks buds opening nearly white, was introduced by Robert Jacques in 1828.

Two historical fiction novels have been written from the point of view of Perpetua. Amy Peterson's Perpetua: A Bride, A Martyr, A Passion (ISBN 978-0972927642) was published in 2004, and Malcolm Lyon's The Bronze Ladder (ISBN 978-1905237517) in 2006.

"See that pot lying there?" she asked her father. "Can you call it by any other name than what it is?" "Of course not," he answered. Perpetua responded, "Neither can I call myself by any other name than what I am - a Christian."

Naming Africa

The following map illustrates the five provinces that North Africa was divided into by Roman administration. (The Romans of course did not rule Ethiopia or Nubia, in East Africa.)

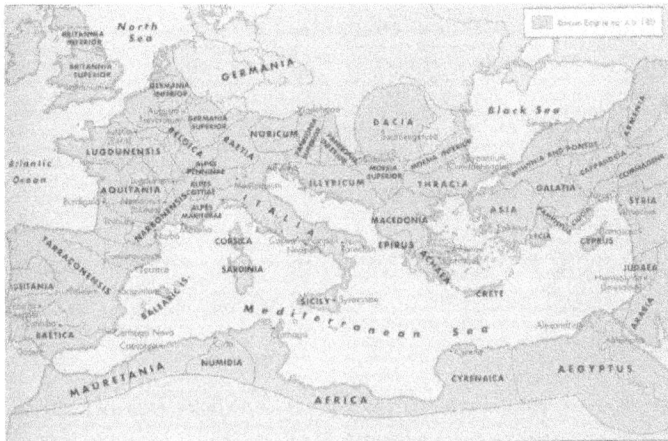

Carthage was in Africa, the province that took its name from the local Afri tribe. Over time, this name held sway as the name of the whole continent.

The ancient name of Africa was Alkebulan. As in *Alkebulan* - "mother of mankind". This name is the oldest – the indigenous - word of origin. It was used by the Moors, the Numidians, the Khart-Haddans (Carthagenians), the Nubians and the Ethiopians. The continent was named "Africa" by the ancient Greeks and Romans. From an Afri-centric perspective, this is a misnomer.

St Augustine was of Berber descent from Hippo. He was born and raised 200 miles from the sea, but spoke only one language – Latin.

Mauretania is obviously different from the modern country by that name. But this civilization grew to be a major force on the west coast of Africa – beyond the pale of Rome.

To the south of Roman dominion were various African tribes. For example, the Lawata, sandwiched between the Roman provinces and the desert. They worshipped

Hammon-Baal, the ancient god of the Libyans and Carthaginians. Remember that Carthage started as a Phoenician (i.e. Lebanese) colony.

Clement of Alexandria

The famous bishop of Alexandria is not to be confused with his namesake, the bishop of Rome, sometimes called the third pope.

Numbering the popes did not start with St Peter but with his successor Linus, who is called the first pope - from 67 – 76 AD. Then came the second pope Anacletus from 76 – 88 AD. He was followed by Clement I, who was pope from 88 – 99 AD. He was contemporary to Polycarp, bishop of Smyrna – who followed St John in Asia Minor. Another contemporary of his was Ignatius, in Antioch, who was bishop there for a long time, from 70 – 108 AD.

Clement I wrote two epistles to the church in Corinth, although these are not included in the canon of scripture. He is mentioned in scripture in Philippians 4:3. His first epistle was written in 95 AD, possibly before some of the New Testament content was written down.

His namesake Clement actually came to Alexandria to pursue his academic career. His origins were in Greece. So he was actually a missionary in Africa, directing the catechetical school of Alexandria. By his time, Alexandria was the intellectual center of the Greek world.

One of his studies of the Hebrews in Egypt led him to denounce racism, when it is a basis for slavery. His views on the rebellion led by Moses of Jewish slaves anticipated the theology of Just War articulated by St Augustine 200 years later. Remember that this was white slaves rebelling against oppression by blacks.

He returned home to Greece when persecution of Christians broke out in Alexandria around 202 AD. At this time, Rome was the hub of imperial government and military; Antioch was the business hub of the empire; and Alexandria was the intellectual centre – of the whole Roman empire.

Tertullian

So many of the church fathers (and mothers) came from Carthage. Of course North Africa was but one shore of the Mediterranean Sea, which connected the dots of the Roman Empire. So it was part and parcel of the Roman world, and the issues about skin-colour and racial superiority would not resurface for many centuries, until the days of the Slave Trade. The Romans were cruel, but they were not racist about it.

In Carthage, in the Roman province of Africa, Tertullian was trained as both a lawyer and a priest. His arguments broke the force of false charges – for example that Christians sacrificed infants at the celebration of the Lord's Supper and committed incest. He pointed to the commission of such crimes in the pagan world and then proved by the testimony of Pliny that Christians pledged themselves not to commit murder, adultery, or other crimes. He was the first recorded writer to refer to the Trinity.

He challenged the inhumanity of pagan customs such as feeding the flesh of gladiators to beasts. He argued that because there are no "gods" thus there is no pagan religion against which Christians may offend. Christians do not engage in the foolish worship of the emperors, they do better - they pray for them. Christians can afford to be put to torture and to death, and the more they are cast down the more they grow...

"The blood of the martyrs is seed" (<u>Apologeticum,</u> 50)

He died in 240 AD.

Chaeremon and Ischyrion

Under the emperor Decius, Christians in Egypt suffered grievously from persecution in 250 AD. Some Christians tried to flee into the desert of Arabia for refuge. One of these was the aged bishop of Nilopolis – Chaeremon. But it was the last time anyone saw them. Even a search party sent out to find them found no trace of them.

For those who stayed behind, it was no better. One magistrate in Alexandria demanded that his procurator Ischyrion renounce his Christian faith. He was told to make a sacrifice to pagan gods, but he refused. For this he was beaten and then impaled to death.

Origen

In Alexandria, Clement was succeeded as head of the catechetical school by a teenage genius of a mixed (Egyptian and Alexandrian Greek) marriage. As a young man, Origen even castrated himself in a literal obedience to Matthew 19:12 – for the Kingdom of Heaven's sake.

He explored facets of theology that no one had written about previously. At this time, theological issues were highly controversial, and so his reputation was mixed – depending on which faction was commenting on his views. But the catechetical school of Alexandria went on from strength to strength. In the fourth century, it was headed by a man who had been blind since birth – Didymus the Blind. This handicapped African was the first to invent a script that could be read by blind people. He was one of the teachers of St Jerome.

He died in 254 AD.

Cyprian

A new persecution of the Christians began in under Emperor Valerian I, and both Pope Stephen I and his successor, Sixtus II suffered martyrdom at Rome.

In Africa, Cyprian courageously prepared his people for the expected edict of persecution by writing a pastoral letter, and set an example himself when he was brought before the Roman proconsul of Carthage, Aspasius Paternus. He refused to sacrifice to the pagan deities.

The consul banished him to Curubis, modern Korba. From there he comforted to the best of his ability his flock and his banished clergy. In a vision he saw his approaching fate. When a year had passed he was recalled and kept under house arrest, in expectation of severer measures after a new and more stringent imperial edict arrived, demanding the execution of all Christian clerics.

He was imprisoned at the behest of the new proconsul Galerius Maximus in 258 AD. The day following, he was examined for the last time and sentenced to die by the sword. His only answer was *"Thanks be to God!"*

"He can no longer have God for his Father who has not the Church for his mother"

(De unitate ecclesiae)

Maximilian of Numidia

One of the first conscientious objectors, at age 23 he declined to join the military when conscripted. He was from Theveste (Tebessa in today's Algeria). Maximilian's father Fabius Victor had been a Roman soldier before his conversion and that meant that his son was automatically expected to join the ranks of the Roman military as well. But he refused – on the grounds of his religious beliefs. His prosecutors warned him of the consequences and tried to talk him out of his principled stance. But he stood firm. So almost immediately, he was beheaded. His last wish was for his new clothes to be given to his executioner. His father went home from the trial rejoicing that his son did not recant.

He died in 296 AD.

Mennas

Not all Christian young men were conscientious objectors. Mennas was an Egyptian camel-driver who enlisted in the Roman army. His legion was sent to Phrygia in the heart of Asia Minor. Then the persecution of Christians under the emperor Diocletian began in 303 AD. This was the severest period of Roman persecution of Christians. Mennas deserted his post and hid in a mountain cave, in order to escape the Roman cruelty.

He watched helplessly as many Christians were sentenced to death under Diocletian's edicts. Finally he decided that he too must come forward with a public profession of his faith. He waited for the opportune moment which came during the annual games at Coryaeum. He entered the arena unexpectedly, and announced to the spectators that he was a Christian. For this, he was beaten and tortured, but he would not recant. So he was beheaded.

He died around the year 303 AD.

Peter of Alexandria

He became bishop of Alexandria in 300 AD, and was known for his reprieve of Christians who did not bear up under persecution. For some Christians lapsed from their faith only to return later after the period of persecution ended. For this he was criticized for being too lenient.

But the Romans were not the only danger to church leaders. The polytheists of Egypt did not like the challenge of monotheism entering their realm. At one stage Peter had to hide from these foes, when a usurper called Melitius took over his bishopric. But Peter returned to Alexandria and resumed his position. Then under Caesar Maximinus Daia another persecution period began. It would prove to be the last before the conversion of the emperor Constantine, who brought religious toleration to the Roman Empire.

Thus, Peter is known as "the complement of the martyrs" by the Coptic church. He was the last Christian to die for his faith under Roman rule – until North Africa was invaded by the Muslims.

Pachomius the Great

Soon after, in Thebes, some reluctant recruits were locked up by the army. They suffered deprivation. Some Christians took pity on them and brought them food. This intrigued a soldier named Pachomius, who then became a Coptic Christian after his discharge from the army. He became a disciple of Palaemon, an old desert father, from whom he learned austerity and self-denial.

With Palaemon's help, Pachomius established a monastery on the Nile. Pachomius went on to build six monasteries in all, with over 1000 monks – and a nunnery, on the other side of the Nile. It was the first time that both priests and nuns lived under one holy rule – a Christian commune.

He died in 348 AD.

Athanasius versus Arius

At the age of 27, a young deacon who was a native of Alexandria – Athanasius - assisted bishop Alexander at the Council of Nicaea. His influence began to be felt. As a result of this council, the identity of Jesus was agreed to be both truly divine and fully human. The Holy Spirit was also defined to be God.

Five months later, on his death bed, the bishop recommended Athanasius as his successor. Another five months later, he was elected unanimously, and at age 30 he became Patriarch of Alexandria. He was the chief defender of Trinitarianism against Arianism.

The thinking of Arius was that God is utterly transcendent. This sounded a bit too much like Neo-Platonism. So the first Christian emperor, in this new era of an un-banned church, had convened a Council of bishops at Nicea hoping to find some common ground. But the Eastern churches (including the Coptic) remained deeply suspicious of the Nicene Creed.

This was the huge controversy of that era, pitching the best minds of the Western (Roman) church against the luminaries of Eastern Orthodoxy. Constantinople stood at the crossroads of East and West and the first Christian emperors tried to use diplomacy to find compromise. The next council of bishops was at Chalcedon. This led to the establishment of the Monophysite churches – three of them in Africa. (As well as the Armenian and the Jacobite church of Syria.) At the centre of this huge controversy were these two African theologians.

Athanasius' refusal to tolerate the Arian heresy led to many trials and persecutions. He spent seventeen of the forty-six years of his episcopate in exile. If you had to describe his ministry in one word, it would be "tumultuous". During his lifetime he was engaged in theological and political struggles against the Emperors Constantine the Great and Constantius II and powerful and influential Arian churchmen, led by Eusebius of Nicomedia. Thus he came to be known as *"Athanasius Contra Mundum"*.

"Jesus that I know as my Redeemer cannot be less than God"

He died in 373 AD. By that time he had been restored to his bishopric in Alexandria.

St Augustine

He came from cosmopolitan Hippo, in North Africa. As a foodbasket for the capital city of the Empire, it had a thriving Roman presence. There was also a long established Hebrew community there. Then there was "the Third Way" – the Christian community - which Augustine refused to join for decades, in spite of his mother Monica's prodding and prayers.

Geographically, his academic pursuits had taken him to Rome. Theologically, he had travelled through the heresy of Manichaeism, through Neo-Platonism, to Christianity. In 387 AD, on the eve of Easter, he was sitting in a garden, agonizing over two alternative pursuits – honours and riches on the one hand and a life devoted entirely to God on the other. (This distinction seems to be lost in today's Prosperity Gospel.) This precipitated a decision to be baptized, and to return to Hippo to form a monastic community. He was later ordained bishop of Hippo.

Augustine's influence is almost without comparison in church history. For the last thirty-five years of his life, he dominated Christian thought, writing books like his <u>Confessions</u> and <u>The City of God</u>. At the root of his influence was his very personal conversion. An about face. A change of heart and mind. Another great African theologian, David Bosch, wrote: "Christianity that doesn't begin with the individual, doesn't begin. But Christianity that ends with the individual, ends." The basis of social renewal is personal renewal. As a changed person, Augustine set about to change the church and society.

"God loves each of us as if there were only one of us."

He died in 430 AD, as the invading Vandals were at the gates of Hippo.

Cyril of Alexandria

As Patriarch of Alexandria, where he was born and raised, Cyril lived at a time when Christianity had come to the fore as the official religion of Rome, and when Alexandria was at the peak of its influence as the intellectual centre of the world. He was a stern bishop, who engaged the Nestorians over that key theological issue of the time – the divinity of Jesus. Nestorius of Constantinople was the chief protagonist of the other view, that refused to call Mary the mother of God. Cyril saw this as watering down the truth. In this controversy, his opponent was eventually declared a heretic.

Then, with the intervention of some papal diplomacy, a compromise was found to make peace between the factions.

He died in 444 AD.

Deogratias

Redemption took on a whole new meaning under this bishop of Carthage. The city had been seized by the Vandals in 439 AD. Being Arians, for 14 years they did not allow a local bishop to be appointed. Then their leader Genseric relented and Deogratias became bishop in 454 AD.

Then Genseric took Rome and returned from there with many captives who he enslaved. Deogratias set about redeeming the slaves. He purchased their redemption by selling off church assets that had been accumulated – ornaments, works of art, and a cherished gold-and-silver plate.

The number of freed slaves grew so fast that they could not all find lodgings. So bishop Deogratias accommodated them inside two churches (Basilica Fausti and the Basilica Novarum) and started a food kitchen to feed them, until they could manage on their own.

The Vandals made several unsuccessful attempts on his life. Finally, he died of exhaustion in 457 AD. He had depleted himself and his church's wealth to free slaves that arrived from a foreign land. In this respect, he can be regarded as a quintessential African hero of faith.

Shenoute

Coptic Christians call Shenoute "the father of the church of Egypt". One of the desert fathers, based at Atripe in upper Egypt, he was exceptionally stern. He revived the rule of Pachomius – which blended manual labour, liturgical prayer and strict obedience.

Cyril, patriarch of Alexandria, admired and trusted Shenoute, whom he appointed as superior to all abbots of the desert monks. By the end of his life, he had attracted over four thousand disciples.

He died in 465 AD – at age 118.

The Rise of Islam

From the Middle East, Islam arrived like a tsunami, crossing North Africa from Egypt to Morocco. Egypt was invaded within seven years of the prophet Mohammed's death in 632 AD. By the year 705 AD, even the Berber hold-outs were gone. Except in Egypt, there was almost total extinction of Christianity, as well as a pathway into Europe via Gibraltar.

Preaching the gospel is still outlawed across most of this region. Missionary work continues, but it is clandestine. Part of this was the clever way that Islam played Christian factions against one another. The in-fighting of factionalism left the church wide open to this invasion.

Egypt was reduced to about 10 percent Coptic Christian. Between this and Islam, the polytheism of ancient Egypt was buried, in favour of monotheism.

Churches were remodelled into mosques. The relics of St Mark were whisked away from Alexandria to Venice for safe-keeping. That city welcomed the relics by building a huge basilica, which became a major destination for pilgrimage.

The Way Forward

St Augustine faced a personal crisis as he sat in a garden in Rome. Did he want self-fulfilment or self-denial? North Africans had risen to be Roman emperors. (Caesar Septimus spoke Latin with an African accent throughout his career, even as emperor.) Berbers rose to be popes. Egyptians rose to be patriarchs and bishops and abbot-superiors.

Da Timothy Code teaches that overseers and deacons should not be "ambitious for money". They should be humble and selfless. What will happen to Christianity in sub-Saharan Africa when this ethos is replaced with church leaders who want to live in posh houses, drive the most prestigious cars and even have their own airplanes?

Clearly some of the first apostles were well-off. For example, Joseph of Arimathea. He could offer Jesus an un-used tomb, and leave the Levant to emigrate to Brittania with an entourage. But he was not reputed for his wealth – rather for his generosity. He was a member of the Jewish council – the Sanhedrin - and in his missionary work he could relate to the upper echelons of British society. He probably left the Levant under pressure from "high society" for having come out in support of Jesus. He had voted against the death penalty for Jesus and he had approached Pilate to allow Jesus a decent Jewish burial. Sometimes our allegiance to Christ has implications. We may lose popularity, influence, even possessions. We may even be forced into exile.

But as St Augustine concluded in that personal crisis he faced over his two future options, church leaders should choose self-denial and a life of service. Sufficiency means having enough; affluence is a nagging temptation. We do not need surpluses to be bishops or deacons.

In today's world, North Africa is once again a place where to publicly confess Christianity can be hazardous to your health. Muslim expansion out of North Africa creates havoc in the Sahel, especially when young Christian girls are abducted and forced to convert to Islam. There is also an ongoing surge of North Africans into Europe. For example, Algeria – once a French colony – is now the largest country in Africa. It is one of the launching pads for the Islamic invasion of Europe, along with Libya and the Middle East. European countries practice religious tolerance to such an extent that they find it hard to contain the evangelistic intentions of Muslims to convert Europe. The sacrifice and self-denial of Muslims is a challenge to European affluence and secularism.

4. West Africa

Circumventing Islam

It has been noted that the phenomenal church growth of the Roman and Byzantine periods was overtaken quite abruptly by the rise of Islam. Coming from Arabia, Islam did not see the desert as the edge of its territory, like the Romans did. So it pushed deeper into North Africa and right out to the Atlantic coast. It has been noted above (in the section about Prestor John) that the rise of Islam in the Middle East positioned Muslims as "the middleman" in trade with Asia. Communist China's "belt and road" initiative, is the latest incarnation of this effort to bridge Europe and Asia, to bring them closer together in terms of trade – circumventing the Middle East.

So it was that Portugal, parked on the Atlantic coast of the Iberian peninsula, became the launching pad (so to speak) for international exploration. In fact, explorers like Columbus when they sailed west were seeking a more direct route to the Orient (the East). Why would you sail west to find the East? This came from the rise of Science, which abandoned its "flat earth" model for a "globe" model.

But in the century before Columbus sailed west to find the East, Portuguese explorers were probing a pathway to circumnavigate Africa – opening a sea-route to India, and beyond. So it was that they began an "end-run" around Islam, which took them around the long coastline of West Africa.

Uninhabited Islands

As they pushed south and then east by sea, probing the coast of Africa, the Portuguese navigators discovered islands like Madeira (in 1419) Cape Verde (in 1456) and Sao Tome and Principe (1470) – that were uninhabited. Compared to the African continent, these offered the immediate prospect of colonization (i.e. their crude model of economic self-development). These islands also served as a springboard for exploration trips to the nearby African coast, that could penetrate further inland.

In very general terms, Christianity had gone through a number of changes that would affect the church's methodology in evangelizing West Africa. For one thing, monastic life had become very wide-spread. Pioneered by the desert fathers, in places like Egypt, monasticism had blossomed all across Christendom. There were now Augustinians, Dominicans, Franciscans with many zealous friars. Not to mention the sisters too – like the "Poor Clares" (the nuns who composed the female side of the Franciscan order)!

Then there had been the Christian Reconquista of the Iberian peninsula. The Christian states rallied and pushed back the Moors. Islam was displaced from the Iberian Peninsula.

Around the same time of the Age of Exploration was the Renaissance, and that triggered the Protestant Reformation, mainly in Northern Europe. For a century or two, Protestants were busy consolidating their new hold on the church there, and states like Germany and Britain were not yet as wealthy as they came to be later - especially with industrialization.

So the **first wave of missionaries** to West Africa were friars and to a lesser extent sisters.

The second wave came out of the Counter-Reformation, especially the Jesuits. This order became a dominant force in world mission, and West Africa was no exception.

Then came **a third wave** of Protestant missionaries – for example the Moravians from Germany and also Anglicans and so forth. Needless to say, the focus of northern European missionaries was on North America. France had the colony of Lower Canada (i.e. Quebec) and some Caribbean settlements like Louisiana. Germany had colonies like Pennsylvania. Holland had New Amsterdam (later New York). Britain had colonies like Virginia, Carolina and Georgia, and also Upper Canada. The focus of Spain was on South and Central America. So it was Portugal that led the way down the African coast, occupying the uninhabited islands, and eventually circumnavigating Africa all the way to India (where they established a colony called Goa).

All along the West African coast different enclaves emerged – the Spanish in the Canary Islands, the Portuguese in Guinea Bissau, the French in Togo, the British in Sierra Leone and Nigeria, etc. These are just examples, meant to be impressionistic. The purpose of this book is not to be comprehensive, but to be indicative.

Finally after a few centuries passed, **a fourth wave** of missionary activity came along. By this time, the North American colonies were "maturing" and starting to send out their own missionaries too. In this same period, Liberia was established as a place for freed slaves from America to return to, to reverse the ravages of the Atlantic Slave Trade.

The Atlantic Slave Trade

The Portuguese were the first to take a shipload of slaves *as cargo* to the New World. That was in 1526 AD, and the slaves were carried to Brazil, the only Portuguese colony on that side of the Atlantic. This was only 34 years after Columbus discovered America in 1492 AD. By the time Columbus crossed the Atlantic, the Portuguese king had already negotiated trade agreements with several West African states. (That is, to trade on a mutually peaceful basis.)

Spain's Kingdom of Castille had already colonized the Canary islands starting in 1402, and enslaved the native Gaunches. In the previous century - out of the first wave of outreach to West Africa - a mission with a bishop had been established on those islands by the Majorcans, from 1350 to 1400. This happened at the time of the Christian Reconquista – perhaps it was a way of ring-fencing Islam?

The first African slaves delivered to the English colonies in North America actually landed as indentured (i.e. contract) workers – on a par with the Irish. Some slaves landed in Virginia as early as 1619, but it was about 1650 AD before slavery hardened into a caste with the horrible racist dimension that has come to haunt humanity ever since.

It should be noted that both the Portuguese and the Spanish had practiced slavery in the Iberian Peninsula going all the way back to the time of the western Roman empire. Including under the Moors, after they invaded Spain - both Christians and Muslims practiced it. However, it did not yet - at that time - have the racist dimension attached to it. That did not kick in until the mid-seventeenth century.

Furthermore, Africa itself practiced slavery all through this period, and African slaves had been traded inside Africa, as well as exported to Europe and Asia, for centuries. In fact, it is said to be still practiced in some Muslim Saharan countries up to the present day.

One of the facets of missionary work, as time went on, was the Anti-Slavery Movement. Missionaries in Africa provided intelligence to the Abolitionists in Britain and America, to help bring it all to an end. On the ground in Africa, they took on the role of a "Slavery Observatory" – gathering intel. For this reason, there was often significant friction between the colonial officials and the missionaries, especially Protestant missionaries.

The last exports of slaves by sea lasted until about 1898 – out of Angola into Sao Tome. This was long after it was officially outlawed, but as both Angola and Sao Tome were Portuguese colonies, a clandestine trade outlasted the ban of 1833. It was not trans-Atlantic, but it was by sea.

Joao Pinto

Out of the second wave of missionary outreach to West Africa came a black priest from Cabo Verde named Joao Pinto. He was a devoted early missionary in the region of "the rivers of Guinea". As a Wolof himself, he was returning as a missionary to his indigenous people after assimilation to Portuguese culture and religion in Cabo Verde.

This shows that from the earliest times, converts were recruited to be missionaries. By no means were all missionaries Europeans - or white. There was a strong indigenous contingent.

He died around 1590.

Baltazar Barreira

The Jesuit mission in Cabo Verde was founded in 1604. Barreira was a career Jesuit missionary who had already spent thirteen years in Angola. He came to West Africa to focus on the Sierra Leone peninsula, via Cabo Verde and Guinea Bissau. He started his new work at Port Loko at age 60! He died twenty-one years later in 1612. His work there was carried on sporadically by other Capuchins and Jesuits, including some amazing indigenous missionaries like Signor Joseph.

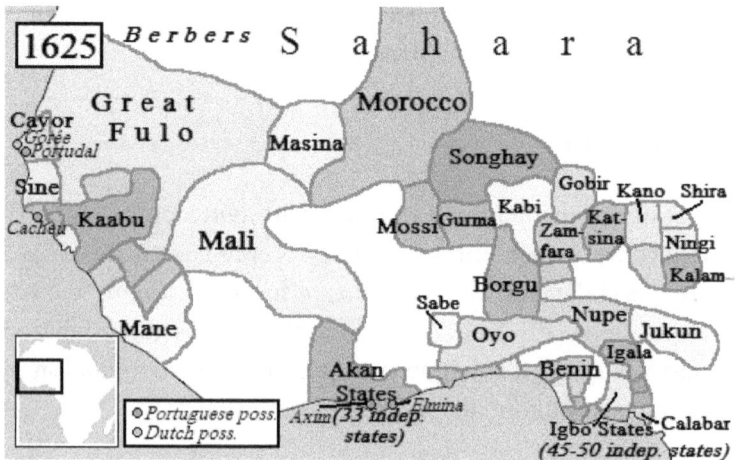

Indigenous Missionaries

A Jesuit visitor named Antonio Vieira gave this glowing report of the work of indigenous priests in 1652:

"Here there are clerics and canons as black as coal, but so grave, so respectable, so learned, such great musicians, so discreet and so temperate that they could arouse the envy of those we see there in our own cathedrals."

Dual Citizens

In terms of the third wave of outreach to West Africa, it was not unheard of, though a bit uncommon, for Europeans (mostly men) to settle in Africa and marry locally. In many cases, the fathers of *mulato* or *mestico* children tried to offer their sons the best of both worlds. Often they were sent off to Europe to get an education, and then returned to Africa. Here are a few examples:

- **Jacobus Elia Johannes Capitein** was adopted by a Dutch trader and taken back to Holland as a child. He studied at the University of Leiden. He was ordained as a minister in the Dutch Reformed Church and returned to work in Elmina for the last five years of his life. He did some translation of texts like the Lord's Prayer into Fante. But he was discouraged from marrying locally. He died in 1747.

- **Frederick Svane** was the son of a Danish father and a Ga mother. He studied at the University of Copenhagen in 1735 and married a Danish wife. They returned to Gold Coast for a time, then settled back in Denmark.

- **Christian Protten** was the son of a Danish soldier who married a cousin of the King of Popo (between present-day Benin and Togo). After his education in Denmark, he returned as one of the first two Moravian missionaries in sub-Saharan Africa – to Accra. He died on the Gold Coast in 1769.

Dual citizens like these, from mixed marriages, experienced the chronic ambiguity of being caught between two worlds. It is reminiscent of St Augustine's conundrum as he sat in that garden in Rome. His roots were in Africa, albeit Roman Africa where he only ever spoke Latin. Then he urbanized to the eternal city. But something kept pestering him - that child's voice outside the wall was a game-changer. It led him to a moment of decision – not to choose the way of affluence and comfort, but to return to Africa and start a monastery. Or a mission station. To plant a church. To start a school or a clinic...

Reverend Thomas Thompson

In 1752, Africa's first Anglican missionary was sent to the Gold Coast (today's Ghana). After four years he returned to Britain because of ill health. His ministry had concentrated on local people rather than British colonizers. He took three boys back to Britian to be educated there. Two died, but Philip Quaque survived. He was the son of Birempon Kojo of Cape Coast.

Philip was ordained a clergyman, and returned to Cape Coast in 1766. He worked there for 50 years, until he died in 1816. He laid a foundation for today's educational system in Ghana.

The Cost of Discipleship

The first Nigerian Christians were just a few Bini converts, in the early sixteenth century. One of them – Afonso Ames – ran a school where a prince became literate in Portuguese. But it would take two hundred years before a Benin king would be sympathetic to Christianity. But his interest was superficial and did not result in any structural change.

In the kingdom of Warri, in the Niger delta, Augustinian monks arrived in the 1570s, from Sao Tome. They converted the king's heir, who ascended to the throne in 1597 – the first ever Catholic "Olu". He thus is called "Dom" Sebastian. His son studied at the University of Coimbra, and all Olu's until 1848 were practicing Catholics.

Like Roman Africa, though, the penetration of European influence did not go very far inland. It was a long string of missions along the West-African coast. Gradually, it began to move north towards the Sahara desert, only to find an Islamic barrier. For the desert had not kept the Arabs and Muslims from coming south of Roman Africa.

The early missionaries might have seen the Benin Wall – the "Iya" as it is called in the Edo language. This 16 000 kilometers of earthworks stood for 400 years, during medieval times, protecting its inhabitants from invasion. That is four times longer than the Great Wall of China! It contained more material than the Great Pyramid of Cheops! Maybe they saw the Benin bronzes, too, before they were carried off to the British Museum? (Benin city is in southern Nigeria – not to be confused with present-day Benin.)

Here is what a Portuguese ship captain Lourenco Pinto observed in 1691:

"Great Benin, where the king resides, is larger than Lisbon. All the streets run straight and as far as the eye can see. The houses are large, especially that of the king, which is richly decorated and has fine columns. The city is wealthy and industrious. It is so well governed that theft is unknown, and the people live in such security that they have no doors to their houses."

The Gospel did not penetrate deep into the interior of Africa by Western missionaries. Herbert Tuwell, an English missionary bishop in Nigeria wrote in 1895: *"As evangelists we are a failure. I do not know of one successful European evangelist"*. For linguistic and cultural reasons, the best evangelists were indigenous ones. This was recognized by all four waves of Christian outreach to West Africa – the mendicant orders, the Jesuits, the Europeans (like Herbert Tuwell), and the American missionaries. Converts were trained and deployed to spread the good news.

Immunity was another factor. Over the decades and centuries, Africans had built up immunity to local disease. It is true that Europeans brought some dreaded foreign diseases to Africa that took a terrible toll. It is equally true that missionaries came to Africa knowing full well that their lives were in danger. Probably a majority of career missionaries died there. They lay down their lives for the privilege of serving Africans. This is often overlooked in all the rhetoric about colonialism and the Atlantic Slave Trade. Well deserved as those critiques may be, it is equally true that missionaries laid down their lives for their cause.

Oddly enough, in the fourth wave of outreach to West Africa, some American missions deployed African Americans as missionaries, supposing that they would be more resistant to local diseases. White churches in America recruited black missionaries for work in West Africa. This health supposition has never been substantiated in medical terms, but it explains the disproportionate number of African Americans among mission cadres. Two black missionaries deserve honourable mention:

- **Thomas Keith** left the West Indies in 1839, soon after the emancipation of the slaves. He worked his passage back to Africa with the aim of telling his own people the good news. How's that for putting your freedom to good use?!

- **Andrew Cartwright** – born a slave – was deployed by AMEZ (the African Methodist Episcopal Zion Church) in Liberia. Born into slavery, he died in perfect freedom.

Locally, the biggest impediment to recruiting indigenous men to work in mission was the monogamy policy. There was a total embargo on plural marriages. This made men shy away from opportunity – to avoid being disloyal to existing wives. Some even sent different wives to different churches so they would not be detected! It was hard for them to understand when they read about patriarchs in the Old Testament who were polygamous and still walked with God. In short, this was a big ask. Not to mention celibacy! But it clearly falls into line with the call to self-denial, as opposed to self-enrichment.

In a book called <u>Missionary Shepherds and African Sheep</u> (Daystar, Ibidan, 1971), West African author Timothy

Bankole wrote: *"The hope for Africa is that Mercedes-Benz cars, large bank balances, political power, large and well-furnished houses and all the other outer trappings of materialism may not ... choke the spread of the Gospel."*

The following eight biographical sketches are as factual as we could find, and rely heavily on Wikipedia as the source. It is not our intention to diminish the bishops or pastors, but to draw attention to an apparent paradigm-shift.

Benson Idahosa

Idahosa is called the father of Pentecostalism in Nigeria. He founded the Church of God Mission International. Since his death, the church has been run by his only son. The church has founded a Bible institute, a children's hospital, and even a university.

According to Wikipedia: *"A claim made by Idahosa that he had raised eight people from the dead was dropped when challenged by the Advertising Standards Authority, who sought evidence that the individuals concerned had in fact been dead."*

He died in 1998 AD.

Bishop David Oyedepo

Oyedepo is presiding Bishop of the megachurch Faith Tabernacle in Ota, Ogun State, Nigeria, and Living Faith Church Worldwide, also known as Winners' Chapel International. He is a college-educated preacher, Christian author, businessman, and architect. He is Chancellor of two universities. Forbes estimated his net worth in 2011 at $150 million USD.

His church owns several buildings including in Britain and the USA, and has four private jets.

According to Wikipedia: *"David Oyedepo Ministries International (DOMI)... is the umbrella organisation comprising Living Faith Church World Wide (a global network of churches); World Mission Agency (WMA - the global missionary arm of the church's operations); Dominion Publishing House (the publishing arm of the church); Covenant University; and the Social Development Missions projects - made up of hospitals, maternity homes, schools, etc.*

"Oyedepo has criticised corruption in Africa as a whole and poor leadership in government."

One can only wonder if Bishop Oyedepo would consider the early apostles to be "winners" or "losers"?

Enoch Adeboye

Adeboye is a Nigerian pastor, General Overseer of Redeemed Christian Church of God in Lagos. According to Wikipedia: *"Adeboye is considered a preacher of the Prosperity gospel, a claim he does not deny, saying that 'Pentecostals have such an impact because they talk of the here and now, not just the by and by... while we have to worry about heaven, there are some things God could do for us in the here and now.'"*

Chris Oyakhilome

Oyakhilome is president of LoveWorld Incorporated, also known as Christ Embassy, based in Lagos, Nigeria. According to Wikipedia: *"He also held the largest single night event held in Nigeria in 2005 with 3.5 million people in attendance "Good Friday Miracle Night... He had over 1.2 million followers on Twitter in 2013, over 1.9 million followers on Facebook, and operates a smartphone messenger called KingsChat."*

"In 2011, <u>Forbes </u>estimated Oyakhilome's personal wealth as between $30 million and $50 million."

T B Joshua

The late TB Joshua was the leader and founder of The Synagogue Church of All Nations (SCOAN), a Christian megachurch that runs the Emmanuel TV television station from Lagos, Nigeria. He has been described as "the Oprah of evangelism".

According to <u>Forbes</u>, Joshua was Nigeria's third-richest pastor – as of 2011.

Matthew Ashimolowo

A Nigerian clergyman, Ashimolowo converted from Islam to Christianity at age 20, then studied at Bible school. He is now the senior pastor of Kingsway International Christian Centre (KICC) in London, earning 100 000 pounds sterling as his annual salary. According to <u>Forbes</u>, his net worth stands between $6–10 million.

The charity behind KICC was investigated for financial irregularities. Changes in governance were mandated by the Charity Commission of England and Wales, and Ashimolowo had to return 200 000 pounds (the equivalent of two years' salary).

The separation of powers is mission-critical to nonprofits. A new governance structure of trustees that the executive branch is accountable to helped to make KICC more transparent. When church resources are "cornered" by executives, what you have is "Church Capture".

Lazarus Muoka

Muoka is the founder and General Overseer of The Lord's Chosen Charismatic Revival Movement. It is one of the most popular churches in Lagos, Nigeria.

But Muoka is not without his critics. Miracles that he performed were called "stage-managed" and "fake" – implied hypnotism and deception. One investor has complained that he was short-changed of millions. A woman also came forward with some noisy allegations.

Chris Okotie

Okotie is the pastor of the Household of God Church International Ministries, a Pentecostal church in Lagos, Nigeria. According to Forbes, he had an estimated net worth at USD $3–10 million in 2011.

He has run for office in Nigeria as well, without success to date.

According to Wikipedia: *"When the government of Nigeria declared the reopening of churches in August 2020 but made it compulsory for members to put on their nose masks or face shield, Pastor Okotie condemned the idea of using face shield claiming it would be a reversal of the veil that was broken on the day Christ died and therefore creating a separation between men and God. "*

Cohabitating with Islam

The importance of Islam to West Africa cannot be understated. Major cultural and academic centres like Timbuktu are located deep in the interior. In the 21st century, it is France, not Spain, that is organizing a kind of Christian Reconquista. France has moved on from having Christianity as a state religion and is now a "secular state". It is using this new identity to try to control the rising tide of Islam.

This is not only in France, but in West Africa too. Most French colonies were across the Mediterranean Sea – like Algeria and Tunisia in North Africa. South of these states are West African states like Mali, Burkina Faso and Mauritania. France and the EU are having to ramp up their military commitment in countries such as these because of the hit-and-run activities of Muslim terrorists even into northern Nigeria.

France may see the military and political challenges. Christian mission needs to be aware of the strong presence of Islam, including its fundamentalist forces, and to assist with a kind of Christian Reconquista. Terrorist groups that have been defeated in the Middle East are popping up in other places, like post-Gaddafi Libya. Unless they are fenced in, they will disrupt West Africa in future. It has already started.

Once again, there is a vivid contrast between the fanatical self-denial of Muslim fundamentalists and Christian trending to affluence and even opulence.

5. Central Africa

From Desert to Jungle

If desert is the predominant landscape of North Africa and West Africa, this changes to jungle and savannah in central Africa. This is a vast area, and there were diverse colonial ambitions to try to "tame" it (Portuguese, British, Belgian and German). For example – by building railroads. At the "scramble-for-Africa" conference in Berlin, the British were dreaming of a Cape-to-Cairo railroad. This was at odds with the Portuguese who occupied Mozambique at the mouth of the Zambezi river, and wanted to open up an east-west corridor across Africa to Angola on the Atlantic side. The eight-century-long alliance between Britain and Portugal reached its low point at this time, because of this conflict of strategic interests.

Pre-WWI Germany also had major colonies in East Africa (e.g. Tanzania) and on the Atlantic coast (Namibia). But it is not the remit of this book to touch on every African country, let alone every missionary or church leader. We can only offer a small sampling, to support our contentions.

By the 1950s, railroads were inter-connected. You could travel east from Lobito, Angola on the Benguela railroad; north from South African cities; or west from the Indian Ocean ports of Mozambique (Maputo, Beira, and Nacala all had rail links). All these railway lines converged on the copper belt in Shaba, the southern province of Congo (and north/central Zambia). However, countries north of the Congo basin like Gabon and Central African Republic were beyond the reach of this rail network – and accessible only by road.

One small vignette comes to mind. As missionaries arrived in ever-increasing volumes, schooling for "mish-kids" became an issue. One solution that emerged was a school called Sakeji, which was launched in Northern Rhodesia (i.e. Zambia). Several generations of the children of missionaries have attended this school – from across central Africa. Alumni from the 1950s and 1960s can attest to the fact that they could travel safely to school in Zambia - by rail - from South Africa, Zimbabwe, Angola, and so forth.

Sadly, the infrastructure has now aged and its functionality is no longer at the same level. But there are on-going efforts to make central Africa cohesive through efforts of "regional integration". Many church denominations have a regional archbishop somewhere, with national bishops in each country and a network of churches - across the region. Representatives from all "branches" meet periodically, in huge conferences.

But Central Africa is just so huge that mostly, churches were planted in one sphere or another with relatively little regional integration. Some entry-points were Atlantic ports, others were Indian Ocean ports. Very few would foot it all over the region – like David Livingstone did. He marched north from South Africa, across the Kalahari to Victoria Falls. Then out to Luanda on the Angolan coast, where he stayed at the British embassy, recovering from malaria. And then back east to Mozambique, and from there to the north

into Malawi and Tanzania. On a follow-up expedition -
looking for the source of the Nile by travelling up the Congo
river - he died in northern Zambia, deep the heart of central
Africa – attacked by a lion.

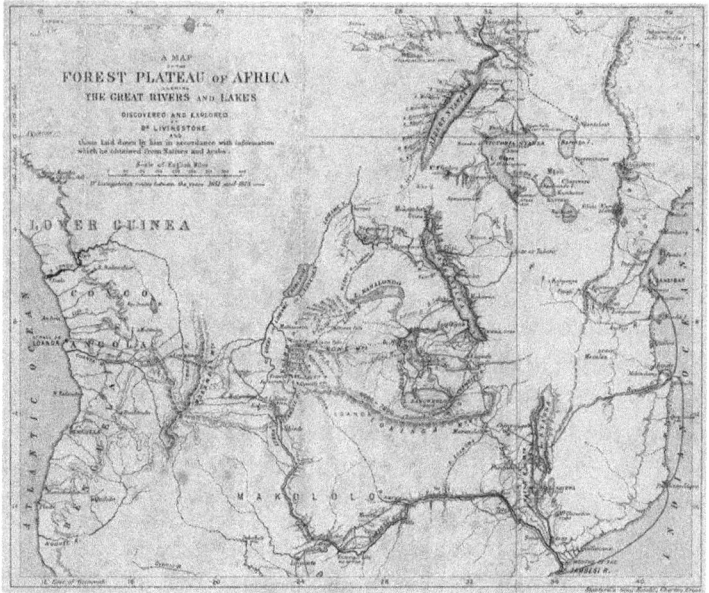

This map is not accurate (it never was), but shows how
much territory Livingstone explored. And at the northern tip
of Lake Tanganyika, he was getting very close to the source
of the Nile in the Rwenzori mountains – only a few hundred
kilometres north of there.

Bakongo outreach

The Portuguese first anchored off the mouth of the Congo
river in 1483 AD. This was five years before Bartholemeu
Dias circumnavigated the Cape. So the navigators were still
probing their way along Africa's coastline. At that time,

there was no distinction between "Angola" south of the river and "Cabinda" north of it, as we have today. This split of the Portuguese colony among the Bakongo only occurred at the council of Berlin. The Belgians, or more precisely King Leopold himself, claimed the Congo river basin as his colony (read: his ranch). They/he needed a window onto the Atlantic shoreline, so he was granted a "space" there at the mouth of the Congo river. Although for centuries by that time, the Portuguese had interacted with the Bakongo kingdom – both north and south of the river mouth. Only from that time was there a European "space" created at the river mouth.

The Bakongo capital was Soyo. The Bakongo king was Nzinga a Nkuwu. This tribe was receptive to Christianity. So the king adopted the Christian name of "Joao I". The capital was moved inland to San Salvador. What gradually emerged was a kind of synthesis of the two cultures. The further inland you went, away from the capital, the more African and the less European this mix would be.

In 1645, the Capuchins arrived, giving a fresh impulse to the original missionary outreach.

Portuguese and Bakongo cultures had a lot in common. For example, they both lived in a daily awareness of the supernatural. But there were some serious issues – like polygamy. In this case, it was agreed that only one spouse was the wife. The rest were concubines.

They both practiced slavery as well. But the slaves of the Bakongo were other blacks – mostly the Jaga. This led to an uprising or jacquerie in 1658, when the capital was invaded and its churches burned down. Forces outside the Bakongo kingdom were getting stronger.

Mbemba Nzinga

The king's son succeeded him after he died in 1506. He adopted the Christian name Afonso. He himself became very proactive in Christian outreach.

He later sent his son off to Portugal to study – who returned 13 years later as a bishop. Mbemba Nzinga ruled until he died in 1543.

By this time, the Jesuits had learned to speak Kikongo. Eventually, they published a catechism in that language, in Lisbon in 1624. It is thought to be the first book ever printed in a Bantu language. Bible translation and vernacular literature are mission-critical to Christian outreach. But of course, these are predicated on literacy, and most sub-Saharan tribes used an oral, as opposed to a written, conveyance of history and learning.

Outreach into Angola

Further down the coast, going south, the Portuguese had found an excellent port at the mouth of the Cuanza river. Here they founded Luanda. This river formed an island where ships could find safe mooring. The Cuanza river drained a high plateau of Miombo woodland – south of the tropical rainforest inhabited by the Bakongo. This was optimal terrain for colonization by an agrarian economy like Portugal. It was better suited to their kind of farming.

Further south, the Portuguese found another great natural port site at the mouth of the Catumbela river, draining the mountainous area inland to the east. Here they built the port of Lobito. From this point, the Benguela railroad was eventually built into the interior, although for the first few centuries, Portuguese settlements remained mainly along the coast.

In 1571, Angola was started as a private proprietary colony – along the lines of Virginia. The founder was the grandson of Bartolemeu Dias, who had circumnavigated the Cape 83 years earlier, in 1488. Paulo *Dias* de Novais founded Sao Paulo de Luanda in 1576 AD.

It has been noted that the Jesuit missionary Baltasar Barreira had spent 13 years in Luanda before relocating to West Africa (Sierra Leonne) in 1589. So the Jesuits were present right from the beginning of this new colony.

By 1665, the Angolans had hatched designs to subdue the Bakongo kingdom. This led to a battle at Ambuila. After that, "Portuguese West Africa" (later called Angola) was ruled from Luanda. The Bakongo were no longer ruled from Soyo but from Luanda. Some of the "separatism" of Cabinda today is rooted in this history of conflict.

Mussa Alebik

It has already been noted that the Portuguese discovered islands strategically located off the coast of Africa. As they explored the east coast of Africa, they found an island where an Arab trader had settled. He was "Mussa Alebik" or King Mussa. This explains the etymology of the name Mozam-

bique, which in the early centuries was just called Portuguese East Africa.

This island is near to Nacala, which is a magnificent natural
port. The Portuguese built their first fort on the east coast on
the "Ilha de Mozambique", as it is known today. This was in
1505 AD – seventeen years after Dias circumvented the
Cape. This is quite far north of the Zambezi delta – getting
towards the Arab zone of influence, centred at Zanzibar.
That island, strategically located just off the coast of the African mainland, had been colonized by the Arabs.

Then in 1508, another port was built at the mouth of the
Pungwe river called Sofala (today's Beira). This is to the
south of the Zambezi river delta. These ports served to provision ships bound for Goa on the west coast of India. Opening a reliable sea-route to the Orient was a higher priority to
the Portuguese than occupying Africa. The African possibilities only came to light later. In the same way, Capetown was
established to provision Dutch ships on their way to the East
Indies. African development came as an afterthought.

The Dominicans worked in both these halting ports. They
received generous support from a Javaneze woman –
Violante. Charities in Africa are so often established with
foreign resources. But then they always encounter the same
challenge – local sustainability.

The Mwene Mutapa

The Zambezi river was navigable for some distance into the
interior. The Portuguese established trading posts at Sena
(160 miles upriver) and Tete (320 miles upriver). They were

now entering the domain of the "Monomutapa" as he is known today.

The Great Zimbabwe was abandoned around 1500 AD, perhaps because the gold had all been extracted? But the Shona ruler remained a force in what today is Zimbabwe.

The Jesuits pioneered mission work in the Zambezi valley, and there was a Jesuit mission to the Mutapa court in 1561. It was successful, in so far as the Mwene accepted baptism. But this caused a backlash from the Muslim traders in the area. A Jesuit missionary was killed.

In response, the Portuguese tried – and failed – to defeat the Mwene by force (from 1569 – 1572). The Jesuits retreated with the Portuguese into Mozambique. But from 1577, the Dominicans returned to the highlands. But one Mwene complained that the Dominicans spent nine months a year trading, and only three months a year as missionaries! This wry remark reflects the perpetual challenge of mission sustainability.

Sustenance was clearly an issue to pioneer missionaries. Among the first of the missionaries deployed by the Church Missionary Society (founded in 1799) were a joiner, a blanket maker, and two shoemakers. For its first 30 years, 31 percent of CMS missionaries were artisans or retailers. The proportion was even higher for the London Missionary Society at 34 percent. The famous missionary Robert Moffat (father-in-law of David Livingstone) was a ploughman's son, who had apprenticed as a gardener. Even St Paul was a tentmaker! There is no shame in recruitment or deployment of enterprising cadres who could find ways to support themselves and their outreach work. The risks of being attacked by a lion or bitten by a malaria mosquito were always high – cadres were needed who were resilient survivors. Many missionaries experience periods of deprivation and illness. For some, the call to Africa could be read as a death sentence.

David Livingstone

David Livingstone started his missionary career in South Africa – that is mentioned in the next chapter. But his focus shifted here to Central Africa in the 1850s. In 1856, he visited Sena and Tete along the Zambezi river near the Indian Ocean. On page 415 of his <u>A Popular Account Missionary Travels and Researches in South Africa</u> (published that year), he wrote: *"None of the natives here can read, and though the Jesuits are said to have translated some of the prayers into the language of the country, I was unable to obtain a copy. The only religious teachers now in this part of the country are two... natives of Goa... During the period of my stay a kind of theatrical representation of our Saviour's passion and resurrection was performed."*

Let's put this in context. According to Mia Couto, a Mozambican academic researcher, the number of Africans – across the whole continent – who had attended High School by the year 1940 AD was less than 11 000. By that time, the continent's population was 191 million. It is now 1.2 billion. One can understand why literacy and foundation education were among the highest priorities of mission work. The other top priority was health. Mission schools and clinics grew up like mushrooms all over the continent.

One of many Livingstone biographers - Alvyn Austin - writes: *"For a generation and more, Livingstone was 'the*

Saint of the British Empire'. Biographies poured forth and rarely mentioned his less congenial traits. The man and the legend inspired generations of men and women, like Alexander Mackay and Mary Slessor, to dedicated missions work throughout Africa.

"During the anti-colonial 1960s, Livingstone was debunked: he made only one certified convert, who later backslid; he explored few areas not already traveled by others; he freed few slaves; he treated his colleagues horribly; he travelled with Arab slave traders; his family life was in shambles - in short, to many he embodied the 'White Man's Burden' mentality."

It would be hard to compare such a confusing biography as Livingstone's to some of the pastors of super-churches in the 21st century. Their success is measured in fame and fortune. Whereas Livingstone had cut his teeth as an African explorer as a missionary doctor in Kuruman, just south of the Kalahari desert. So he was well aware of the African narrative... It has often been noted that when the white man came to Africa, he had the Bible and the Africans had the land. He preached to them and invited them to convert to his God. So they closed their eyes to pray. When they opened their eyes, somehow, he ended up with the land while they got the Bible!

Livingstone had seen this narrative playing out in South Africa, and he was part of the solution, not part of the problem. He attained fame, to be sure, but never fortune. After his explorations from Quelimane, into what we now call Zambia, Malawi and Tanzania, he launched another expedition in 1866, sponsored by the Royal Geographical Society. He headed up the Congo river – right into the warm heart of central Africa. Four years later, he reached the Burundi shores of Lake Tanganyika. So much time had passed, that it was feared that he might have perished. So the <u>New York Herald</u> sent out an American search party – led by Henry Stanley – to find out what had happened to him. In 1871, Stanley found the great explorer in Ujiji, Tanzania. Possibly the most famous words ever uttered in Central Africa were: *"Dr Livingstone, I presume?"*

Livingstone kept exploring – he wanted to find the source of the Nile. He was getting very close to it when his life ended, 18 months later – in a lion attack. *"Africa is not for sissies"*.

Was he the saint of the British Empire? Or had his ego been inflated by a "messiah complex", fed by his popularity? One thing Livingstone did manage to do, was to raise awareness about the massive opportunities for economic development in Central Africa. And this vision was predicated on the need for literacy and education – a role that in those days was still understood to be largely the remit of missionary work.

The Comber family

Thomas Comber first served in the Cameroons for three years, with the Baptist Missionary Society. Before returning on furlough to Liverpool, he made a reconnaissance trip up the Congo river. Returning to Britain, he raised support to start a mission among the Bakongo. Before starting out, he got married. The newly-wed Minnie Comber reached San Salvador in 1879. Although she enjoyed the trip up country, she died within a few weeks of arrival.

Her sister, a missionary in the Cameroons, died in 1884. Comber's brother – also a missionary in the Congo – died in 1885. In 1887, Thomas Comber himself died.

This family vignette has been repeated time and again, in every African country, down through the centuries. "Blackwater fever" was public enemy number one (now called malaria). This occupational hazard was embraced by foreigners in a spirit of solidarity with their indigenous target groups.

Heli Chatelain

As was the case in West Africa, the first two waves of Catholic missions were followed by two more waves of Protestant missions – first from Europe, and later from America. Angola has already filled a whole book on church history – A Igreja em Angola by Lawrence Henderson. Then each denomination has its own "folklore" about its missionaries, mission stations, mission schools and hospitals, and related humanitarian projects – sometimes in the form of books. Then there are biographies galore – taking us through Congo, Mozambique, Zimbabwe, Zambia, Malawi, and so forth. One of the best known of these is The Poisonwood Bible by Barbara Kingsolver.

We will only feature one early missionary here – a Swiss pastor named Heli Chatelain. He came to the central highlands of Angola basically as an observer with the Filafrican Mission. Not an election-observer, which would only come a century later. But of slaving. Because this horror continued out of Angola and into Sao Tome long after it was outlawed internationally. Nor was this a "trans-Atlantic" trade, because the distance from the Angola coast to the island of Sao Tome was not far.

75

Now the Cadbury family were British industrialists famous for their chocolate. They bought a lot of the raw materials from Sao Tome. And they were a Christian family. They got wind (from missionary observers) that slave labour was still being used on the plantations of Sao Tome - as late as 1898. They threatened to boycott Sao Tome. And they also encouraged more missionaries to serve in Angola, where they could bring this clandestine trade to an end.

In his marches around central Africa, David Livingstone had also occasionally met up with caravans of slaves. But mostly his encounters had been along the Zambezi river – headed out to the Indian Ocean coast. (Probably to destinations in Arabia, via Zanzibar.) He would confront them, as a British diplomat (one of several hats that he wore). He would report them. In our day, missionary work still includes whistle-blowing against corruption and patronage. This is an integral part of church outreach, as it always has been. "No justice, no peace".

Chatelain died in 1908 AD, in Switzerland.

Dr Walter Strangway

In September 2020, Dr Stephen Foster of Lubango, Angola, was contacted by government protocol. Another Canadian doctor, Steve Collins of Huambo, Angola, was also contacted. They were both invited to attend the opening of a new government hospital. The General in charge of the Office of the President of the Republic explained: *"You are an invited guest of the President at the official opening of the Dr Walter Strangway Hospital tomorrow morning at 10 o'clock in Cuito, Bie. "*

Dr Foster and Dr Collins were provided with air travel to the grand opening, where the President cut the red ribbon. A few days later, Dr Foster filed this report:

"A month ago, an old friend Dr Campos, a former Dean of the Faculty of Medicine with whom I had worked 30 years ago, who is a member of the Congregational Church of Angola with long links to the United Church of Canada, had called me to say that they would like to ask me to say a few words on behalf of medical missionaries efforts here in Angola that date back 140 years. This would be at an opening Ceremony of this hospital at a date to be determined and organized by the churches in Central Angola. I told him my colleague Dr Steve Collins had grown up knowing Dr Strangway and had called him Uncle Walter and that wouldn't it be more proper for Dr Collins to speak?

"Nothing more got said and I figured it was off due to Covid 19 restrictions preventing travel outside Luanda for those inside the sanitary cordon of Luanda. Clearly, I didn't know the Powers of the President.

"I was met by State Protocol and asked to wait for the new Dash 8 bought from Dehavilland some 4 months ago. At 16:45 we were on our way to Cuito. Opposite me were 3 members of the President's office one of whom took me to supper that evening. He was Chief of Social Media for the office of the President a very friendly and engaging chap. He plied me with questions about our 42 years here. I didn't spare him any of the details of the lengths to which his ruling party had sought to make enemies of the church and in particular how we missionaries had been variously accused of working for the CIA, gun running, rhino horn reselling, diamond smuggling, gold digging, and most recently selling

human organs procured from innocent rural folk to be re-sold in Namibia with Mission Aviation Fellowship based in Guelph ON, serving as the delivery mechanism. I told him that bringing us in from the cold is going to be a long process of relearning to trust one another again. At that point I figured if I was being offensive, so be it. I kept asking him if the President was serious in getting the churches involved again in Health Care?

"I was up at 05:00 penning a speech as they still hadn't said what was going to happen at the Opening Ceremony. I wondered if we would get a chance to meet. A helicopter was scrambled at 07:30 to get Dr Collins from Dondi mission 130 kms away, where he was doing a Cataract surgery field trip. He has been doing this for 25 yrs now and has helped more than 20,000 Angolans recover their sight with the simple technique of lens extraction and intraocular lens placement. The previous evening he had refused to come by road as he said he needed to do the post op care and bandage removal on the eight newly operated patients from Friday. He told the Chief of Protocol if the President really wants me send a Helicopter!

"By 09:30 we were taken in a car with the Canadian flag in the windshield to the new Provincial Reference Hospital. There we met with our Honorary Canadian Consul Allan Cain. He is also Director of Development Workshop and a 40 yr veteran of Angola too. We shared notes. He had been given 24 hours notice as he needed a rapid test for Covid to be able to travel outside Luanda. He said after much Internet research he hadn't been able to uncover a connection between the State President and Dr Walter Strangway, but there was a persistent gap in the story from birth in 1954 to

1972 when he entered the clandestine activities of the MPLA and became a soldier.

"Just before the President walked down the red carpet a lady from the President's office drew all three of us aside and said the President has asked to meet us after the tour of the hospital in the Governor's Palace. Please be ready for the pickup vehicle. Finally I thought we might get his ear - something I've wondered often, when or if, would ever happen.

"The Ceremony started with a video on the life of Dr Strangway born in Petrolia ON, a University of Toronto MD grad, who with wife Alice a Lab Technician, left Ontario in 1928 and worked at a place called Chissamba, 60 km from the provincial capital until 1967. He built a 140 bed hospital doing some 40,000 operations. In addition, as a reflection of his holistic thinking, he set up 42 primary care points before the advent of antibiotics and vaccines. The colonial regime didn't permit any Protestant work within a 15 Km radius of any town. I found it difficult to believe that State media was broadcasting a paean praising a medical missionary after having being treated like a pariah for so long.

"The tour of the Hospital found us in a first world place of 230 beds. It was if we had been beamed up to the donor Spain's backyard. Some 47 million Euros later, over two years, a beautiful place is ready. It will need just 170 doctors and another 800 plus staff to begin to use it. At present there are 17 largely Cuban specialist MD staff.

"What a preparation into our 'Audiência' with the President who did indeed give us a half hour of his time. After intros Dr Collins asked what is the connection to Dr Strangway?

He smiled and said, let me tell you my story. The next 15 minutes we were spell bound as it emerged that his father had been a nurse trained at the Methodist mission hospital of Quessua near Malange about 400 km due east of Luanda. After 1953 his dad got a job with the Port of Lobito clinic where indeed the President was born in 1954. His dad got picked up by the secret security police known as PIDE in 1958 and jailed for two years in Luanda. Upon release in 1960 his CV was blackballed preventing him from working in any state institution ever again. His father found employ at the Chissamba Hospital and a warm welcome from Dr Strangway. During his boyhood then the President watched Walter on rounds as his dad insisted he do his homework under supervision often on the porches of the wards. The President spoke with such affection and emotion one could see he was deeply moved by those events of many years ago. He said he hoped that someday there would be an opportunity to honor Dr Strangway. Saturday the 12th of September, 2020 - some 5 days from what would have been his 121st birthday - was that day.

"I couldn't have prepared a more perfect moment to be asked by our Consul to present a vision of what the next ten years in Angola could look like. I said: "Sir, if God should spare me for another decade to be the age of my colleague Dr Collins I would like to prepare up to a 100 new Doctors, Nurses, Admin folk and Mid-level providers capable of bringing health care at the primary and secondary level to the rural peoples of Angola. We need your permission to launch a pilot "skunk works" program admittedly at first in only 4 municipalities. Once proof of concept, costs, impacts on health indexes etc, then generalization to other areas can be carried out.

"Angola has drunk the 'wine of Cuba' for too long - at that he smiled. We are shackled to inappropriate models of health care delivery whereby without 40 different specialists present in a hospital nothing happens. We need polivalente generalists in the second line of care, able to handle 80% of the traffic. They would refer appropriately, instead of inundating our tertiary care hospitals with floods of primary care needs.

"I said further: 'Sir, we in the churches of Angola have had our hands tied. Undo our handcuffs please'. He smiled! I said I have been here for 42 yrs and my other Christian colleagues up to ten years and none of us have been recognized by your Angolan College of Physicians and Surgeons. Please allow us to work!

"He asked what all this would cost – that is, to train Human Resources, to rehabilitate broken hospitals and create the Teaching hospital over the next decade? I said 25 million USD would get us started. He turned to his cabinet chief and said, 'That's only 2.5 million per year. Let's do it. Please get Dr Foster's contact details.'"

Did I mention that Dr Steve Foster is a third-generation career missionary in central Africa? And that he is also an alumni of the above-mentioned Sakeji school (in northern Zambia) for "mish-kids"? He is the Albert Schweitzer of the 21st century.

Uebert Angel

Usually called the Prophet Angel, he is described as a pioneer of the modern-day prophetic movement. He is a Zimbabwean, who teaches that a pastor should not rely on the offerings of his flock, but on other business ventures. This could be biblical "tentmaking" or an excuse for his penchant for business in the UK.

His holding company Angel Organization is now using the trade-name The Billion Group. Its centrepiece is a property investment company called Sam Barkeley Construction. That subsidiary owns properties valued at $20 million in six countries. Other subsidiaries include a bank, Atom Mobile, Picasso hotels and some resorts.

The value of his own home in the UK is estimated value of between $2 – 4 million. He drives a Lamborghini and his wife drives a Rolls Royce. His net worth is estimated at $50 million.

The flamboyant preacher of The Spirit Embassy: The Good News Church - in the UK - has a reputation as both a philanthropist and a philanderer. For example, on a Sunday in May 2013, Prophet Angel handed one of his followers the keys to a brand new Range Rover Sport worth over US$100 000. That's not all! That car had personalised number plates: "PSALM 23:5".

His charity the Uebert Angel Foundation has delivered aid to Zimbabwe and other African countries as well. Prophet Angel has become a mentor to a number of other preachers of the prosperity gospel, including the three profiles that follow…

Prophet Shepherd Bushiri

According to Wikipedia: *"Shepherd Bushiri also known as Major 1 or Prophet Shepherd Bushiri, is a Christian preacher, motivational speaker, author and businessman from Malawi. He founded and leads a Christian non-denominational evangelical church known as the Enlightened Christian Gathering.*

He is currently under investigation – again - for fraud, money-laundering, and embezzlement. The amounts exceed R100 million (about $6 million). In a related affidavit, he states that he earns R566 000 ($33,333) per month. Also, two women have accused him of rape.

After his initial arrest in South Africa, he skipped bail and fled back to Malawi (even though his passport had been seized). So South Africa applied for extradition – which the Malawi courts have respected with some reluctance.

Wikipedia says that *"Shepherd Bushiri is now known as one of the wealthiest pastors in the world and one of the most affluent people in Africa.*

Bushiri is mentored by multimillionaire businessman and leader of Good News Church in UK, Prophet Uebert Angel. Bushiri is said to be the most celebrated and popular Spiritual Son of Prophet Angel."

His net worth in 2021 is estimated at $150 million. How did he get so wealthy? Here is a scan of his investment portfolio:

- His preaching and live appearances generate his baseline income
- He owns a number of properties, hotels and resorts
- He owns interests in several mines
- He has a fleet of four private planes

But what is heretical (as in simony) is his sale of "Jesus blood" at R200 per vial. This puts him in the class of the proverbial *snake-oil* salesman.

Isaiah Brian Sovi

Sovi is another "spiritual son" of the Prophet Angel. He was born and raised in Kitwe, Zambia. He started law school but never finished, choosing instead to go into the ministry.

He is the leader of Imperial City Church, a Pentecostal ministry that was founded in 2015. He has been described as a "pastor-preneur" because of his dual role as preacher and business tycoon. He owns IBS Holdings with subsidiaries IBS Cargo and IBS mentorship. He has written a book called Biblical Forex Trading.

He has been reputed to perform miracles. Nevertheless, as these claims were unproven, and he was caught money-laundering and operating illegally, he was closed down in Botswana, for a time.

Apostle Miz Mzwakhe Tancredi

A K A "the Ironman", Tancredi is another "spiritual son" of the Prophet Angel. He is described as the "owner" of the New Life Church in Vaal, South Africa.

In 2017 he launched a book in Sandton called Command Your Success. At this event, billed as a "business and relationship seminar", he and his wife Charisma Tancredi were described as "South Africa's latest power couple".

Tancredi is also billed as a healer: *"Ailments once thought incurable are being cured in the name of Jesus Christ, cancer, HIV AIDS."*

Since the time of Jesus, faith-healing has been part of outreach ministry. We do not question the authenticity of this spiritual gifting. However, any direct relation to wealth-generation must be tested for simony. And there is a big difference between sustainability and opulence.

The Price of Discipleship

There has been a subtle shift from "the cost of discipleship" to *the price* of discipleship. One has a sense that the modern-day prophetic movement is trying to "re-invent the church". As in the early church there are family connections, mentorships and outreach linkages that help the movement to grow.

In medieval times, especially in the run-up to the Protestant Reformation, there were some very materialistic popes in Rome. They were clearly "ambitious for money" and still remained popes. But this focus led them astray – for example, into the selling of indulgences to raise money for the mother-of-all-churches, the Vatican. It led on to the practice of simony, which rankled a young priest named Martin Luther.

Central Africa is a resource-rich region with great weather for agriculture. In such a setting, no one needs to remain in poverty. This was clear to the pioneer missionaries and explorers – like David Livingstone. Perhaps their sincerity got entangled with colonialism to the point that it did more harm than good?

However, we maintain that *Da Timothy Code* is still the best advice for church leadership. It is perennially relevant, and when bishops, deacons, prophets and healers arise who do not align with it, we get suspicious. They will probably dismiss our suspicion as jealousy? The readers can decide for themselves.

By dying ignominiously on the cross for us, did Jesus fail or succeed? Can you imagine Jesus of Nazareth driving a Rolls Royce? Would he wear big rings on his fingers and flashy clothes? Was his role as *messiah* one of a CEO, or a suffering servant?

6. Southern Africa

Each chapter in this book is a collage of faces... They have been set out in sequence, as a way of relating what transpired from the earliest times until the most modern times – by region. Not by narrating a plot, but by presenting a stream of icons. The timeline in South Africa is the shortest of all, but there is no shortage of vignettes to choose from. Again, the selection is not comprehensive – it is just a sampling. Our purpose is to get a message across – *"Ask not what your flock can do for you. Ask what you can do for your flock."*

Krotoa

She was born in 1643 - nine years before the Dutch arrived to establish the Cape Colony. 155 years had passed since Bartholomeu Dias first circumvented the Cape of Good Hope, in the early days in the Age of Discovery. So for over a century, this sea-route to the Orient had been in use. The Dutch finally decided to establish a permanent stop-over point for provisioning at what is now Capetown.

Slave trading had already begun in West Africa by the time of Krotoa's birth – but that coast was much closer to America and the Caribbean. It would still be a century before the Abolitionists emerged, and 152 years before the London Missionary Society was founded in tandem to that. Meanwhile, the focus of the sea expeditions to the Orient was still exploration and trade. Only after the LMS got into gear would that narrow focus expand to include philanthropy, development and empowerment.

Krotoa was born as a member of the Strandlopers tribe. They were sedentary, non-pastoral hunter-gathers. They are believed to be one of the first clans to make acquaintances with the Dutch people. She was the niece of a Khoi leader and trader called Autshumato. Her uncle was a clan leader and Krotoa's fate and fortunes were closely aligned to his. Prior to the Dutch's arrival Autshumato served as a postal agent for passing ships of a number of countries.

Circumstantial evidence suggests that at the time of the arrival of the Dutch, Krotoa lived with her uncle Autshumato (also known as Harry by the Dutch). At the age of 11 or 12 she was taken in to work in the household of Jan van Riebeeck, the first governor of the Cape Colony. There are multiple accounts of how Krotoa came to work under the household of Jan Van Riebeeck. One account paints the story of how the Dutch forcefully kidnapped the child Krotoa, however no hard evidence confirms this account. Krotoa was taken in as a companion and as a servant to Riebeeck's wife and children.

Assuming that Krotoa had been living with her uncle, then Krotoa's early service to the Dutch may not have been as violent a transition as it is sometimes made out to be. It is believed that the first baby born to chaplain/healer Willem Barentssen Wijlant and his wife - coupled with the rapid spreading of a virulent disease in the settlement - sparked the initial negotiations to obtain services from a local girl. As Autshumato had a long history of working for Europeans, it is believed that the Dutch first turned to him for negotiations. It is quite plausible that he offered up his niece for servitude in order to better his standings with the Dutch.

So as a teenager, she learned Dutch, Portuguese and French, and like her uncle, worked as an interpreter for the Dutch who wanted to trade goods for cattle. Unlike her uncle however, Krotoa was able to obtain a higher position within the Dutch hierarchy as she additionally served as a trading agent, an ambassador for a high ranking chief and a peace negotiator in time of war. Her story exemplifies the initial dependency of the Dutch newcomers on the natives who were able to provide reasonably reliable information about the local inhabitants.

On 3 May 1662 – when she was 19 years old - she was baptized by a visiting parson, Petrus Sibelius, in the church inside the Fort de Goede Hoop. The witnesses were Roelof de Man and Pieter van der Stael. She was the first indigenous southern African to be baptised a Christian, and so that is when the Dutch settlers named her "Eva". In this same year, Zacharias Wagenaer (who was German) arrived at Cape Colony and replaced van Riebeeck as governor. Van Riebeeck left the Cape immediately.

On 26 April 1664 – at age 21 - she married a Danish surgeon by the name of Peter Havgard, whom the Dutch called Pieter van Meerhof. She was thereafter known as Eva van Meerhof. She was the first Khoikoi to marry according to Christian customs. There was a little party in the house of governor Zacharias Wagenaer. The keeper of Wagenaer's diary noted that it was "the first marriage contracted here according to Christian usage with a native." As it was only twelve years after van Riebeeck's arrival at the Cape, inter-racial marriages were not yet prohibited.

In May 1665, van Meerhof was appointed superintendent of Robben Island, so they left Capetown. That same year, the Castle of Good Hope was built. Krotoa's family briefly returned to the mainland in 1666 after the birth of her third child, in order to baptize the baby. Van Meerhoff was murdered on a slaving expedition to Madagascar in 1668.

After the death of her husband came the appointment of the fourth governor of the Cape Colony – Jacob Borghorst. This governor held extremely dim views of the Khoi people. Because at this point the Dutch settlement was secure, he didn't find a need for Krotoa as a translator anymore. So the widow Krotoa returned to the mainland in September 1668 with her children - unemployed. For a while she remained a respectable member of European society, but began to suffer from alcoholism. Now in her late twenties, she left the Castle in the settlement to be with her indigenous family in the kraals. In February 1669 she was imprisoned unjustly for immoral behavior at the Castle and then banished to Robben Island.

Krotoa returned to the mainland more than once just to find herself banished to Robben Island again. In May 1673 she was allowed to baptise another child on the mainland. Her two children fathered by van Meerhof - Pieternella and Salamonwere – were adopted out after she was banished. They were eventually taken to Mauritius in 1677.

Meanwhile, Krotoa died on 29 July 1674 and was buried on 30 September 1674 in the church in the Fort. She was only 32 years old. She is noted as one of the most written about women in South African history, with her name appearing in the journals of the Dutch East India company from as early as 1652.

After her death, Krotoa's story would not be deeply explored for nearly two and a half centuries. Instead, attention was mostly put on white European women who came to South Africa on missionary expeditions. It was not until after the 1920s that her story became a part of South African history.

- The novel *Eilande* by Dan Sleigh (1938), translated from Afrikaans by Andre Brink (in Dutch: Stemmen uit zee/in English: Islands), describes the lives of Krotoa and her daughter Pieternella from the viewpoints of seven men who knew them.

- As late as 1983, under the name of Eva, she was still known in South Africa, as a caution against inter-racial marriage.

- In 1990, South African poet and author Karen Press wrote a poem entitled *Krotoa's Story* that attempted to reimagine Krotoa's life, emotions, and conflicting desires partly from her perspective. The poem was based on an earlier children's story by Press entitled *Krotoa*, which was created as part of an educational initiative by the South African Council for Higher Education designed to inform schoolchildren about colonization from the perspective of indigenous South Africans.

- In 1995, South African performer Antoinette Pienaar created a one-woman play entitled *Krotoa*. The work was first performed at the Little Karoo National Arts Festival, where it was awarded the "Herrie" prize. The play is unique in its depiction and memorialization of

Krotoa as a mother to the nation, a symbolization which had been previously rejected by white South Africans.

- In her essay "Malintzin, Pocahontas, and Krotoa: Indigenous Women and Myth Models of the Atlantic World", University of Michigan professor Pamela Scully compared Krotoa to Malintzin and Pocahontas, two other women of the same time period that were born in different areas of the world (Malintzin in Mesoamerica, Pocahontas in colonial Virginia). Scully argues that all three of these women had very similar experiences in the colonialist system despite being born in different regions. She reflects on the stories of Malintzin, Pocahontas, and Krotoa and states that they are almost too familiar and resonate so comfortably with a kind of inevitability and truth that seems, on reflection, perhaps too neat. Therefore, she claims, Krotoa is one of the women that can be used to show the universality of the way that people were treated in the colonial system worldwide.

- Most recently of all, the full-length feature film *Krotoa* is a made-in-South-Africa motion picture, released in 2017. Its slogan is "caught between two cultures about to collide".

Krotoa's life story should be as inspiring to missionaries as it is to women!

For the initial arrival of the Dutch in April 1652 was not unilaterally viewed as negative. Many Khoi people saw their landing as an opportunity for personal gain as middle men in the livestock trade; others saw them as potential allies against pre-existing enemies. At the peak of Krotoa's career as an interpreter, she clearly held the belief that the Dutch presence could reap benefits on both sides.

It is not fair to always characterize indigenous people as seduced or coerced and the arrival of foreigners as the prelude to "cultural genocide". For example, there is circumstantial evidence that Krotoa showed consistent hostility to her Sandloper clan and even to her own mother, who lived with them. Why can't people – *for their own reaso*ns – choose the approach they prefer?

Clearly, in some settings, this choice was the rejection of any foreign interference. But in Krotoa's case, one can note:

- She learned three foreign languages (Dutch, Portuguese and French)
- She converted to Christian faith (she was baptized, and she also baptized her children. She was also buried in a church.)
- She married a white settler (and had perhaps the first "Cape Coloured" children?)
- She chose to remain in South Africa, not to emigrate
- She kept in touch with her roots
- She had a career (other than the sedentary hunting and gathering of her clan of origin)

The alcoholism that she suffered from is so, so sad, and yet so predictive. In her life, there were periods of stable marriage and parenting, as well as periods of what used to be called "back-sliding". In short, she was human. Four centuries later, the abuse of substances is still all too common among youth.

Life was both good to her, and hard on her. At the end of the game, we should be congratulated for *playing well*, more than for winning.

There is good reason to call Krotoa the mother of South Africa! Almost 400 year later, white men still find black women to be attractive, and yet it is not easy to find one another deeply through all the resistance on both sides.

About a century after she was buried in the church at the Fort in Capetown, her remains were removed and buried elsewhere in an unmarked grave. That was her ultimate exile. But in 2016, her bones were moved again - back to their original resting place.

The Hottentot Code

Slavery did not just go away – it adapted into other forms. In the USA, "convict leasing" emerged soon after the Civil War. In the Portuguese colonies there was *"trabalho for-cado"* (forced labour). And in South Africa there was the Hottentot Code. The Khoi were compelled to work on settler farms, or alternately to join the military. This was double jeopardy – for they were already being dispossessed of their tribal lands.

To their credit, missionaries were a force against this prevailing policy of colonialism. Including, of course, the actual malpractice of slavery – long before it was outlawed.

There is a misconception that the Bantus entered the north-east corner of South Africa about the time that Europeans arrived at the Cape. Archaeology suggests otherwise. The Bantus had arrived far earlier. And so had explorers from India – especially down the south-east coast of Africa. There is evidence of a strong Indian influence embedded is Swazi culture - in the country that is now called eSwatini. However, one can generalize to say that blacks had come down the east coast all the way to the Eastern Cape, where the Xhosas settled (one of the Nguni tribes). These are distant relatives of the Zulus, the Swazis, the Ndebeles, and the Shangans.

Although there was some co-habitation of land by the Khoi, the San and the Bantu tribes, one can generalize that the Khoisan lived in the drier west of South Africa, and the blacks lived in the wetter east. This explains to some extent why the first interaction between Europeans and indigenous people was with the Khoi around Capetown. The Xhosa even lived on the west bank of the Fish river, but were driven back by the Dutch settlers as they moved eastward. That river became the eastern boundary of the colony. The northern boundary was the Orange river. Remember that policies were set overseas, and the seat of local government in Capetown was simply there to administer and enforce them. Naturally with the help of the military.

The fact is that Capetown itself changed hands more than once between the Dutch and the British. That had to do more with European wars than African wars. Eventually, though, the British gained the ascendancy, and took definitive control of Capetown in 1806. The Dutch name of Riebeekstad was dropped. Exactly twenty years after that (in 1826), one generation on, the Afrikaners organized the Great Trek –

across the Orange River and its main tributary the Vaal river, into what was called the Transvaal. In the manifesto that the Afrikaners used to recruit Boers for this trek, one point listed was to get away from the "liberal" influence of the missionaries!

George Schmidt

Because Capetown was founded by the Dutch and eventually conquered by the British, missionary outreach really started in earnest with the Protestant effort, not so much with the Catholic orders and the Jesuits. They did arrive in later years, but the pioneer missionaries in South Africa came mainly from Holland, Germany and Britain - until they were reinforced by the American missions. The Huguenots cannot go unmentioned – they were French Protestants basically escaping the persecution of the Counter-Reformation (i.e. the Inquisition). They were the followers of John Calvin who rose to academic prominence in Paris, before moving to Geneva. They came to South Africa via Holland.

The first Moravian missionary – George Schmidt - arrived in 1737. Soon a mission station had been established a few days trekking inland from Capetown – called Genadendal (Valley of Grace). Schmidt died in 1778, and the next surge of Moravian missionaries arrived in 1792. During this period, mission stations increasingly became an early version of "refugee camps" because so many Khoisan were being displaced by the influx of settlers into the interior. Some voices aver that these centres of technical training for the Khoisan simply supported the colonial policy of trying to create a cheap labour force with some skills, for the new trending of urbanization.

By 1850, the population of South Africa was 400 000. By that time, sixteen thousand Africans lived on 32 mission stations. We can only conclude that these growth points were a mixed blessing, providing some literacy training, some skills development and of course evangelization and translation of the scriptures into the vernacular. But the motivation for doing this was distinct from the colonial agenda.

A cynical view of missionary outreach was that it piggy-backed on colonialism, being hard to distinguish at times from the Boer expansion. Tom Hiney answered that critique in his book On the Missionary Trail, on page 329: *"It is hard to see how men like Johannes Vanderkemp, who married the widow of a Madagascan slave and had assassination attempts made on him by white settlers, could in any way be seen as a stooge of imperialism"*.

Johannes Vanderkemp

In 1779, a Dutch doctor named Johannes Vanderkemp fell in love. He was an aristocrat and she was a wool-spinner. When news of this "unsuitable marriage" reached the Dutch court, he was summoned before Prince William V to explain himself. In due course, he lost his cherished wife in a traumatic boating accident, and later moved to South Africa, where he found that inter-racial marriages were also "unsuitable". Nevertheless he married the widow of a slave.

Upon his arrival in Capetown he politely rebuked clergymen who kept slaves. He visited a Moravian mission as part of his short orientation period. Then he set out to reach the Bantus on the Eastern Cape. For a time, he stayed under the watchful eye of the Xhosa king Gaika, but there were no converts. However, one person he did influence profoundly was Ntsikana – one of the king's advisers. Only after Vanderkemp's death many years later did Ntsikana convert to the Christian faith.

Vanderkemp made two attempts to start mission schools for the Xhosa on the Eastern Cape, but there was so much resistance from the white settlers that the governor of the Cape Colony recalled him from that frontier. So he started a third school for the Khoi in Graff-Reinett, teaching literacy to slaves. Before long, 300 wagons of armed settlers assembled at Zwargershoek to forcibly send him on his way. They burned his Khoi school to the ground.

So he moved again, to Algoa Bay. His vocation changed too, because these were the days of the anti-slavery movement in British Parliament. As long as Britannia ruled the waves, outlawing slavery could be enforced to some extent worldwide. Certainly it was curtailed, by intel from people like Vanderkemp – who became a kind of Slavery Observatory. He filed his reports with both the Governor in Capetown (Dutch or British, depending on which was holding sway) and also with William Wilberforce, the British MP who was driving the Anti-Slavery Bill.

Vanderkemp's accounts of the horrific ways that the Khoi were being treated by white settlers were popular reading in the anti-slavery media at that time.

Then in 1802, Cape governor JW Janssens insisted that Vanderkemp move his fourth mission further south to Botha's Plain - a less fertile area, of course. This fifth mission station put some space between him and the settlers. He built a mission station there called Bethelsdorp, near present-day Port Elizabeth. It soon filled up with destitute Khoi refugees, who were being dispossessed of their aboriginal lands. Vanderkemp became fluent in the Khoi language. He almost seemed to embrace privation, possibly as a way of doing penance for the boating accident in which he lost his first wife, in Holland.

Missions were best known over the years for their efforts in education and health. Mission schools and mission hospitals can still be found all over Africa. But progress was slow, because of the resistance that missionaries faced from the settlers and business interests invading deep rural Africa. Fighting for justice was always part of the missionary's re-mit, and that included whistle-blowing. They had to expose the excesses of Colonialism.

Venderkemp and Read were summoned to Capetown by governor Janssens, who would not allow them to leave town. That is, until 1806 when Britain reclaimed the Cape colony and installed a new governor – Lord Caledon. He sent an emissary to Bethelsdorp to ask the missionaries to endorse the conscription of Khoisan into captive labour. They refused. In his report to the governor, the emissary Colonel Collins recommended that the mission be closed down on the grounds that is existed "not to benefit the Colony, but the Hottentots". While the governor did not take his advice, the tension between settlers and missionaries did not go away either.

Soon after Lord Caledon was replaced with a new governor – John Craddock – the intrepid Dr Vanderkemp died in Capetown, in 1811. He had survived a number of assassination attempts over the years. He was 63 years old, and had served twelve years as a missionary.

Edward Snowden put it this way: *"The sad truth is that societies that demand whistleblowers be martyrs often find themselves without either, and always when it matters most."* It is good citizenship to report crime. And someone has to speak truth to power.

Ntsikana

This advisor to Gaika, chief of the Xhosas, was the first Xhosa to convert to Christianity. But he moved in that direction very slowly and cautiously – many years after he first came into contact with missionaries like Dr Johannes Vanderkemp at about age 20. Then later in his life, at about age 36, he had further contact with missionaries James Read and Joseph Williams, who taught him more from the scriptures. It was then that he decided to relocate to the Mankazana hills, close to a mission station. From there he and his whole house attended instruction every Saturday at the mission, and stayed over for Sunday morning worship.

When Williams died two years later in 1818, Ntsikana became the worship leader. His Christian influence touched the lives of leaders such as Xhosa King Ngqika, his counsellor, Old Soga (the father of Tiyo Soga), and Tiyo Soga's older brother, Festiri.

Even in Xhosa culture he was already an esteemed prophet and hymn-writer, before his conversion. So he applied these talents to the expression of his new faith. An English translation of his Great Hymn in isiXhosa follows – as arranged by the Rev. John Knox Bokwe in 1875:

The Great God, He is in heaven.
Thou art thou, Shield of truth.
Thou art thou, Stronghold of truth.

Thou art thou, Thicket of truth.
Thou art thou, who dwellest in the highest.
Who created life (below) and created (life) above.
The Creator who created, created heaven.
This maker of the stars, and the Pleiades.
A star flashed forth, telling us.
The maker of the blind, does He not make them on purpose?
The trumpet sounded, it has called us,
As for His hunting, He hunteth for souls.
Who draweth together flocks opposed to each other.
The Leader, he led us.
Whose great mantle, we put it on.
Those hands of Thine, they are wounded.
Those feet of Thine, they are wounded.
Thy blood, why is it streaming?
Thy blood, it was shed for us.
This great price, have we called for it?
This home of Thine, have we called for it?

African culture was never abandoned by Ntsikana, whose faith was more of a full integration of two systems of thought. This hymn is a great example of Christian faith engaging with African life and experience. In this respect he was a precursor of the African-initiated churches that have become predominant among African Christians. He died in 1821.

The Black Circuit

Missionary James Read joined Vanderkemp to found Bethelsdorp mission station in 1802. The two worked closely together until Vanderkemp's death in late 1811.

That same year, a new Cape governor took office - Sir John Craddock. He decided to set up a circuit court at Algoa Bay to investigate allegations raised by the missionaries about atrocities and injustices. In its day, this was the equivalent to our Zondo Commission. It was unprecedented. They called it "the Black Circuit" and only a year after Vanderkemp's death, it had already debriefed a thousand witnesses – European, Xhosa and Khoi. Fifty-eight settlers were put on trial, but everyone knew that for every person on trial, at least ten more went un-reported.

Unfortunately for both James Read and the LMS, James Read impregnated a teenage San girl, which came to light in 1816. This caused a period of turmoil. By 1822, the mission deployed a Superintendant in Capetown of the 15 LMS mission stations, and the ethos of LMS missionaries shifted from the egalitarian approach of the pioneer missionaries to one that was closer to the lifestyle of the settlers. Without condoning immorality, one of the chronic hazards of missionary life had always been loneliness and isolation. In modern times, the Catholic church is dealing with scandal after scandal involving celibate priests. Again, without debating the theology of celibacy, even God once said: "It is not good for man to be alone". Some observers regard inter-racial marriage as the litmus test of racial prejudice. On the other hand, they can present even more challenges than "normal" marriages do.

It is worth noting that when the Cape Folk moved to Kat River in 1829, they invited James Read to be their pastor. This was the first "African-initiated church" without mission roots. These settlers saw their migration as a kind of "Exodus". To them, Kat River was the "promised land". Their schools were named after people like William Wilberforce and Fowell Buxton (who had taken over from Wilberforce as the leader of the abolition movement in British parliament after his predecessor's retirement in 1825). However, the settlement kept getting destroyed in frontier wars, and after three of these trashings, it did not recover. In a period of one century, there were no less than nine wars between the British and the Xhosa.

Moffat

Not all mission outreach was to the east of Capetown, some was to the north. This includes John Kicherer and William Edwards, who had sailed from the UK with Vanderkemp in 1798. They had travelled north – towards the Orange river, but not that far - to work among the San "bushmen" in the northern Cape. The northern frontier at that time was Roggeveld, a plateau in the Karoo. They went beyond that and crossed the river Zak, where they made a first attempt to start a mission – at a place that did not deserve its name "Happy Prospect".

While there, they were invited by chiefs from the more populated Orange river banks to come further north as teachers. But the climactic conditions of that area were so severe, so hot, that there were several false starts – missions founded then abandoned. Also, they were into the territory of Jager Afrikaner, a "Hottentot warlord" who is described in the next section. Their next mission station going upriver was at "Warm Bath".

Further east along the Orange river they entered the territory of the Griqua, a Khoikoi tribe. They continued the classic role of Slavery Observatory. Another mission station was founded there in 1816, at Lattakoo - near to the confluence of the Vaal and Orange rivers. They were now "off the map"

- outside the boundaries of the British colony and always moving deeper into the interior.

In 1817, a Scottish missionary named Robert Moffat arrived and was deployed there. The son of a ploughman, he had apprenticed as a gardener – optimal skills for a pioneer missionary. He went on to acquire skills in building, carpentry, blacksmithing and printing.

In 1818, the mission instructed Moffat to push further east and north into Bechuanaland. After some exploration, another mission station was founded in 1820 among the Tswana. This placed missionaries far beyond the two rivers. Moffat's first three years in South Africa were on his own. Then his betrothed arrived in Capetown and joined him. At Kuruman, he and Mary went on to have ten children.

Moffat was the first translator of the Bible into Setswana. In 1831 the mission acquired an iron hand-press. Moffat used it until he retired in 1870. It continued in use until 1882. He also became a writer and a speaker.

Bible translation was not without its blunders, as pioneer missionaries learned the language without grammars or dictionaries – which they themselves had to generate. Moffat once translated "lilies of the field" incorrectly, so that in Tswana the verse read: "Consider the tarantulas, which toil not".

A missionary doctor arrived at Kuruman in 1841, called David Livingstone. He went on to wed Mary Moffat, the oldest child of Robert and Mary Moffat, in 1845. He assumed a strategic role in the development of the mission but left the LMS – and South Africa – to focus on Central Africa.

Kuruman became a launching pad, from which the missions to Matabeleland and later Central Africa were begun. Eventually, the LMS would also pull out of the Cape and hunker down in central Africa. In 1855, Livingstone "discovered" Victoria Falls and by 1857 he had resigned from the LMS and been deployed by the British government as a consul in Quelimane (near the mouth of the Zambezi river). It was from there that he commanded the exploration of Central Africa, outlined in the previous chapter.

Jager Afrikaner

In the late 18th century, a group of Khoi and former slaves had escaped from Capetown and made their way north beyond the Orange river. They fled "beyond the pale".

This group adopted a Malay name – "Orlam". After the turn of century, their leader was Jager Afrikaner. He had succeeded his father Klaas Afrikaner when he died. He was Khoi, but Cape Dutch was the Orlam language. He had once worked on a Cape farm as a shepherd. This group did not choose between "fight or flight" – they did both! So in the eyes of the settlers, Jager Afrikaner was a "wanted man" – an outlaw. There was a bounty on his head. His people lived by cattle-rusting. There were frequent skirmishes that left the missionaries very vulnerable.

Then - as a result of a dream - he became a Christian. This was not uncommon, as in local culture people still listen closely to their dreams. He dreamed that he was climbing a mountain. The valley below was ablaze with veld fire. As he climbed, he saw a shining figure on the mountain top. The higher he got, the brighter it got. He reached the figure and just when he was going to speak to this vision, he woke up.

105

Jager Afrikaner was converted to Christianity by German missionaries in 1815. He became close friends with Robert Moffat after his arrival in 1817. Moffat took him back to Capetown in 1818 and negotiated amnesty for him with the governor Lord Somerset. Jager Afrikaner was generous to a fault. For example, he once made and eight-week trip to transport the Moffat's personal effects and livestock. On another occasion, Moffat fell very ill and Jager Afrikaner nursed him back to health.

When missionaries left the Orlam, heading further east, he assumed the position of religious leader and teacher. He died in 1823. He was succeeded by his son, Jonker Afrikaner.

Dr John Philip

The London Missionary Society had been preceded by the Moravians, from Germany, but soon took the lead in establishing mission stations in South Africa. One of the first three LMS missionaries in South Africa was the leader of the delegation – Dr Johannes Vanderkemp. He died 12 years after his arrival, in 1811. For the next decade, the LMS kept expanding, in spite of both internal and external difficulties. So in 1819, a delegation was sent out by the LMS to conduct a review. One of the members of that delegation was appointed as LMS Superintendant in 1822 - based in Capetown. He is sometimes referred to as "the Protestant Pope".

One thing he found was that there were 7 000 slaves in Capetown alone. So almost immediately, he launched a slave chapel in the middle of the city, beside the mission house. This was right at the time of the abolition movement, and Britain was gaining ascendancy with its Empire. This is noted to contextualize the expansion of Christianity. While it is true that missionaries used the Pax Britannica as a cover to spread out under, it is also true that missionaries were generally acting in favour of local people – not to colonize them but to evangelize them. In fact, to liberate them. This meant that they not only faced the risks of Africa and the scepticism of local people, but the ire of the settlers and the colonial regimes as well.

Dr John Philip's book about the ill-treatment of the Khoisan and Bantu people was widely reported in the British media. It caused a huge outcry. He corroborated what a parliamentary inquiry had found, although its report had been suppressed. Only because of his book was that commission's report finally disclosed to the public. It corroborated all that he had written, and this caused censorship to be lifted and "An Ordinance for Improving the Condition of Hottentots and other Free Persons of Colour" to be promulgated.

He died in 1851, in Capetown, after serving thirty years as mission Superintendant.

Tiyo Soga

Tiyo Soga was born a Xhosa, in 1829. That was 186 years after Krotoa's birth; and 82 years after Johannes Vanderkemp's birth.

By this time, missions were sprinkled all over the world including Africa and literacy, Bible translation and schooling were their archetypical functions. So Tiyo Soga went to a mission school at primary level, then to Lovedale for high school. At this point, Lovedale was multiracial – but not co-ed!

During the war of 1846 he fled with the Scottish (Presbyterian) missionaries and was then taken to Scotland by a teacher at Lovedale, Mr Govan. (I am guessing that this teacher might have been Govan Mbeki's namesake?)

In 1848, while in Scotland, he was baptized and then returned to South Africa later the same year. He became a teacher in the Eastern Cape. But he had to flee again with the missionaries during the 1850 war. In 1851 he travelled again to Glasgow in Scotland to study for the ministry. In 1856 he was ordained in the Presbyterian Church. In 1857 he married a Scottish women named Janet Burnside. Together they returned to serve as a missionary couple – first at Mgwali for 11 years, then at Tutura for 3 more years until his untimely death.

Willem Saayman uses a very good word to describe the love/hate relationship between colonialism and missions – "entanglement". While missions spread out largely in the slipstream of colonial expansion, the truth is that they were often at odds with business and government interests. Perhaps the best-known instance of this is the abolitionist movement, which sought to bring an end to the Slave Trade. Obviously business interests opposed this on the whole, as did many government leaders. But key Christians like British MP William Wilberforce led the campaign to outlaw it. Missionaries around the world served as "observers" who collected and shared intelligence with the campaign, to bring it to an end. Without these whistle-blowers, it might not have succeeded.

Just as it is unfair to say that native people were coerced into conversion, it is also unfair to generalize that missions endorsed colonialism.

One event stands out in Tiyo Soga's ministry – where he took a stand against the boys in his school taking the rites of initiation and circumcision. He saw this as "back-sliding" into traditional religion, which put him at odds with the parents of the learners enrolled in the mission school. This incident highlights the difficult position that he was in, as a black missionary.

Willem Saayman traces the roots of both African nationalism and Black Consciousness back to the life and work of Tiyo Soga.

Ironically perhaps, he chose to send his own coloured children off to school in Scotland, but on their departure he told them: *"take your place in the world as colored, not as white men, as Kaffirs not as English- men... For your own sakes never appear ashamed that your father was a Kaffir, and that you inherit some African blood"*

Tiyo Soga was the only minister of the time who preached in congregations of all the protestant denominations of that period. So he not only planted seeds of African unity but of church unity as well.

Willem Saayman summarizes Tiyo Soga's influence as follows: *"It can be argued, then, that Soga left a legacy which is important today in the development of Black Consciousness and even pan-Africanism. This dimension of Soga's contribution flowed from his concern about the quality of life of his people in the oppressive colonial context. Because of this basic concern for people, Soga served as a symbol of unity already in his lifetime. As a loyal Presbyterian minister until his death, Soga can be seen as the role model of generations of African church people to come after him, people who were (and are) both consciously Christian and consciously African."*

The word "ambivalence" is used by Saayman to describe Tiyo Soga's way of living with the "entanglement" of colonialism and missions. It is a word that could well be used to describe Krotoa's attitudes as well. She tried not to take sides, so to speak – she could see that engagement could be mutually beneficial to both sides.

Opposition came from both sides. The attitudes of whites towards Tiyo Soga were often openly racist and if there ever was a missionary caught between two worlds, it was Janet Burnside Soga! Yet when her husband died, in 1871, she did not race back to Scotland. She went to live with *his* mother for a period, at her village, so that all their children could become proficient in Xhosa before returning to Scotland. Then they returned to Scotland to complete their education. Only one of those children remained there for good. The others all returned to South Africa – including a doctor, a veterinarian, a magistrate, a teacher and a pastor. They worked in different settings including mission stations.

Of the four boys among those siblings, three paid their mother the high complement of also marrying Scottish women, and the other married a black South African.

If the proof of the pudding is in the eating, then there is no doubt that Tiyo Soga's inter-racial marriage served as an anchor for his "ambivalence" – which steered towards church unity, Pan-Africanism and Black Consciousness.

Reformed Church Missionaries

In the early days, Christian outreach in South Africa followed the same pathways as elsewhere – mission stations, Bible translation, schools and hospitals, etc. But in South Africa, the term "missionary" gradually developed a new and different connotation. This is because the settlement by Europeans happened on a much more massive scale. Much of South Africa started to look pretty much like any country in the North, in terms of infrastructure and urbanization.

In their own way, the "boers" or farmers were - and still are - deeply religious. Every town that sprung up built a church with a steeple. All the farmers attended these Dutch Reformed churches and they all were visited by their pastor, from time to time. That is, the man who preached on Sundays in their church – to them. In their farm homes, they typically kept a "parson's lounge" – used only on these visits. Otherwise, they lived their day-to-day life in the farm kitchen.

But every church also had a "missionary". Another man, whose role was to evangelize "the blacks". So when the pastor halted his horse and buggy in front of the boer's house on a pastoral visit, he was always accompanied by another white man, who would not go into the farmer's house, but would rather meet with all the black farm workers.

You can give some credit to other mission efforts just as they operated in all African countries, but in this country, it was different. White people went to church and every church supported a "missionary" as well as a pastor. To a very great extent, they are the ones who have made South Africa what it still is spiritually – a place where God is worshipped widely. By all races.

There is a yeast in Bible teaching that does not rise at first. But all that teaching to black farm workers had a subversive effect. They wanted to read the Bible, and that meant learning how to read. There was always this implicit risk – in evangelization, in literacy training, in education. Willem Saayman often spoke about "the chickens coming home to roost".

Much later, in 1977, an African-American preacher called Leon Sullivan of the Zion Baptist Church (in Philadelphia) introduced a list of principles that American companies operating in South Africa could use to ratchet up the pressure against apartheid. Because by law, up until that time, blacks were unable to hold supervisory positions in the work place. This was getting to be un-sustainable, and the corporate sector realized it. By the 1980s, the Sullivan Code was that yeast – and it started to rise…

Subversive Subservience

UNISA publishes a series of books called "*African Initiatives in Christian Mission*", to celebrate what has been accomplished and to balance the number of books which have been written about foreign missionaries. Without a doubt, more books had been written about foreign missionaries like David Livingstone than about indigenous missionaries like Tiyo Soga. In this book about *Da Timothy Code*, we have tried to find a balance between both. But UNISA has done a great service to correct the imbalance.

One such African leader was ZK Matthews, the first black school headmaster in South Africa. Literacy and education had always been paramount in mission work, so the emergence of a black headmaster was very significant. His example and its implications are sketched in the following clips:

"An African leader such as ZK Matthews adopted some of the dominant tropes of the humanitarian-liberalist missionary discourse. I am thinking here especially of dimensions such as the call for equal justice before the law, the value of education, and so on. In this respect one can therefore speak of him as being subservient to Western missionary hegemony, and 'following the script'..

"He seldom openly challenged white missionary hegemony directly, but provides evidence of having contributed to the 'escape' of the message from the hands and minds of white missionaries. In this respect he therefore existed and acted in a manner subversive to white missionary hegemony.

"We have failed to recognise that the missionary journey had much more in common with the flight path of the boo-

merang: no matter how hard and how straight it is thrown away, it never follows a straight line. If thrown with skill, it always returns... Peter goes to evangelise the 'pagan' Cornelius, and returns to his exclusivist judaistic community of Christians forever a changed man. The subversive memory of Jesus alive in the Christian community chronicles throughout that missionary chickens always come home to roost. The unwritten, sometimes even untold history of Christian mission emphasises, over and over again, that true evangelisation takes place only where the evangelisers are evangelised...

"Unless the evangelisers, whether white Africans or white Westerners, are evangelised, we will have labored in vain. We must assist 'the chickens to come home to roost' - in mutuality and interdependence."

Earlier African cries of *Uhuru!* (freedom) turned to *Amandla!* (power) under apartheid. The Struggle was not just for liberation but for empowerment.

Rev. Theophelus Hingashikuka Hamutubangela

He was born on the same day that the Kwanyama king Mandume ya Ndemufayo was killed, in the battle against Portuguese and South African colonial forces at Oihole. His life spans a transition period. After graduating from seminary he became a deacon and later a priest. He also served as a school teacher. He became an activist, petitioning the UN to intervene against unscrupulous labour practices.

His missionary work included political support for the Ovamboland People's Organization, the forerunner of

114

SWAPO. It was set up as a labour organization to fight exploitation.

Although he was harassed by the authorities, repeatedly arrested, imprisoned and even poisoned to the point of paralysis, he lived to see Namibia on its way to a free and democratic future.

Trevor Huddleson

We have already noted Mia Couto's count – that by 1940, the number of Africans across the whole continent who were attending High School was less than 11 000. So we know how rare black lawyers were – *Mandela and Tambo* was the first black law firm ever. It was founded before the Group Areas Act was enacted, because they suddenly found that their office was in a "white area"! Most post-WWII black intellectuals and political leaders emerged from mission schools.

About this time, yet another missionary arrived in Johannesburg from England, named Trevor Huddleston. In 1954 he gave Hugh Masekela his first trumpet. In 1959 he co-founded the Anti-Apartheid Movement (AAM) with Julius Nyerere. He became a bishop in Tanzania in 1960. In 1988 he and Archbishop Desmond Tutu addressed a rally of 200 000 people in Hyde Park, London. By now it was clear that public opinion was evolving. Winds of change were howling. Few missionaries ever got to blow the whistle as loud as Huddleston!

But Africa and Africans have also changed rapidly. There has been much urbanization (a way for investors to enjoy a cheap labour force). The largest church denomination of them all is now Zion Christian Church. It has made huge contributions to both the Christianization of Africa and the Africanization of Christianity. Along with St. Engenas ZCC.

The truth is that many African missionaries now travel out to different corners of the world, and this accounts for the revitalization of the church in those settings. It is not uncommon to find African nationals serving as missionaries in Europe, America or Asia.

In South Africa, the Zondo Commission represents a great leap forward for transparency. Instead of harbouring secrets, citizens of all races are being invited to step forward and come clean on what they know about State Capture. Yet some of them require "witness protection" because of the still-prevalent attitude that they are "*impimpi*" (i.e. snitches). They need the persistence and fortitude of that pioneer missionary Dr. Johannes Vanderkemp, champion of the Khoi.

Just as white whistle-blowers spoke up about settlers behaving badly, so also the time has now come that blacks are openly reporting corruption and patronage committed by other blacks in governance. This should not cause them to be labelled as coconuts or oreos, but as heroes. Democrats.

Father Huddleston died in April 1998 at his home in England. He was 85 years of age. His ashes were interred next to the Church of Christ the King in Sophiatown.

Archbishop Emeritus Desmond Tutu

For some time, the South Africa Council of Churches had a general secretary who had started his career as a teacher. Then when Afrikaans was imposed as the medium of instruction in all schools, he chose a new career path, and went to seminary. He became the first black (Anglican) bishop in South Africa. As general secretary of the SACC, he was invited to visit Denmark, and while there, he was interviewed on television. Although he was a pastor and a theologian, he signaled his support for economic sanctions. Upon his arrival back in Johannesburg, he was visited by the secret police. They gave him 24 hours to publicly retract his statement, which had made the world news.

That night, as he agonized over what to do, his wife Leah said that she would rather see him happy on Robben Island, than miserable at home in Soweto! Women of influence like her include Bonhoeffer's mother and of course Coretta King, who never remarried after her husband was assassinated in 1968.

Tutu did not recant his view. But he was not arrested after all, because of the ecumenical and international support that he commanded. It was just more of the intimidation that church leaders get for speaking truth to power.

So how could an elected President say – at a church conference yet! – that the church should stay out of public life?! Did he want our churches to become like the Reich Church? Heretical in its absolution of government crimes? There has been no genocide in South Africa, but there has been xenophobia, graft, patronage, and waste. And there was an African genocide – in Rwanda – during the years of Mandela's presidency.

No, the church has a mission. The gospel is told and re-told in different settings, situationally. South Africa is well evangelized and deeply religious. Among its greatest leaders were churchmen like John Dube and Albert Luthuli. *The light is shining in the darkness, and the darkness will never put it out.*

The SACC's recent critique of the weakening of the Judiciary by its undermining by the ruling party (specifically a faction of the ruling party) is a vivid example of this light shining in the darkness of state capture.

Andries Tetane

Disparity in South Africa is phenomenal. Driving along the R21 highway from Pretoria to Joburg, I once observed so many huge mansions sprouting up on the hill by Irene Mall, then within minutes the sprawling township of Tembisa. It is graphic to the point of being shocking. Someone described South Africa as a First World Country and a Third World Country occupying the same space.

Andries Tatane was on the right track. There is a *Myth of Spontaneous Development*. Transformation doesn't just happen, it gets kick-started – by facilitation, activism and resources. In fact the word "intervention" actually means that someone has to "come between". So Tatane was out there, protesting the lack of service delivery. There are risks in being a freedom fighter.

This community activist excitedly exchanged SMSes with his wife as a protest was being organized for the next day – over (can you believe it?) **lack of service** by the authorities. The opposite of foot-washing humility is lack of service by those in power. The very next day he was killed by a police bullet! An information officer at South Africa's NGO coalition - Butjwana Seokoma - wrote this reflection:

"I must admit I was still young when former President P W Botha declared the state of emergency in 1986 in an attempt to fight anti-apartheid turmoil. I can still remember the day when I saw members of the South African Defence Force, supported by the Lebowa Police, beating and forcing learners from the surrounding high schools into trucks and police vans, for taking part in a protest.

"Today, I pride myself for being a citizen of South Africa. Under the new Constitution (Section 7), the State is obliged to respect, protect, promote and fulfil the rights outlined in the Bill of Rights.

"However, the events of last week, in which members of the South African Police Service (SAPS) beat and killed unarmed protestor, Andries Tetane, at a close range during a service delivery protest in Ficksburg, is a reminder of the long road the country has to travel in order to realise human rights for all its citizens. There is nothing wrong in protesting against non-performing local governments. However, there is something fundamentally wrong when the police's actions amount to the violation of the protestors' rights.

"I support the South African Institute of Race Relations' view that the beating and shooting of Tetane, who by many accounts sought to come to the defence of others being assaulted by the police, on national television, could provoke a political reaction that government will not be able to contain.

"Tetane's death was brutal, unnecessary and took the country backwards in terms of the promotion and protection of human rights. Frankly, I don't think Tetane's death will de-

ter people from embarking on similar service delivery protests in future. The killing reminds me of the events of 1986."

Andries Tetane was in the right. Citizens have the right to protest, and as an activist that day, he had been busy cajoling police not to use their water canons on disabled demonstrators and the elderly, but on the healthy ones. His sense of justice was and is inspiring.

Ray McCauley

A former champion body-builder, Ray McCauley took on a new challenge – to build up the Body of Christ. He is a protégé of Dr Kenneth Hagin, the late founder of Rhema Ministries in Tulsa, Oklahoma. McCauley founded Rhema Church upon his return from Bible School in Tulsa. As the curtain came down on the apartheid era in 1994, McCauley and Rhema Church participated in various events that helped with the peaceful transition to a democratic nation. So he is held in high esteem as a church elder.

His has written several books, including <u>Expect More</u> and <u>Purpose Powered People</u>.

However, both an acrimonious divorce and his connection to the prosperity gospel have made him a controversial figure in church circles, at times. He is also thought to be sympathetic to the ruling party, rather than speaking with a prophetic voice to power. But he has been an outspoken critic of gay rights.

According to <u>Times Live</u>, he made some pointed remarks about the prophetic movement: *"The CRL Rights Commission did its own investigation into the commercialisation of religion and abuse of people's belief systems and its findings and recommendations were clear ... Their findings embarrassed us."*

"We have seen the exploitation of people and the sexual and emotional abuse of people. All these and many other things have tainted the image of the church and put us in a very bad light."

"Where criminality has been committed, the police must take charge and the law must follow its course."

Timothy Omotoso

According to Wikipedia, this Nigerian clergyman is *"the senior pastor of Jesus Dominion International, based in Durban, South Africa. He is currently in jail and on trial at the Port Elizabeth high court for rape and human trafficking. He is alleged to have groomed his victims and began molesting them from the age of 14."*

Omotoso was arrested by the South African priority crimes unit, the Hawks, in 2017. He has been charged with human trafficking and rape. Over 30 young girls and women from three branches of his church are victims. His two co-accused are prominent women from his church.

The Omotoso defence playbook included an unsuccessful bid in the Supreme Court of Appeal to get the presiding magistrate recused. However, after that bid was denied by the SCA, the magistrate decided to recuse himself.

Omotoso has tried repeatedly to get released bail, but has failed to, presumably because he is seen as a flight risk.

Pastor Ray Macauley's remarks about the prophetic movement are a propos of this debacle.

7. Epilogue

Re-thinking the criteria for sainthood?

We see in the early apostles a "cloud of witnesses" who delivered the Word of God all over the known world. They scrimped and sacrificed. They were revered, so future generations of church leaders kept to the same core values.

So how is it that a church that for centuries cherished and venerated those who were crucified, beheaded, tortured and sawed in half has now switched allegiances to adore and emulate church leaders who are rich and successful?

The profiles of recent African faith heroes in East, North, West, Central and South Africa is an astounding contrast to our church fathers (and mothers) of today.

What has happened to church leadership?

And more importantly - what has happened to church followership?

Prophets or Profits?

How do you square the prosperity gospel with *Da Timothy Code*? I Timothy chapter 3 is unequivocal. Church presbyters and deacons should not be ambitious for money.

In the Old Testament, one of the twelve tribes of Israel was not given land – because they were set aside to be the ministers of Judaism. There was an embedded logic to this – similar to *Da Timothy Code*. Servants of God should not be "ambitious for money". They should receive support from those they serve – adequate but not excessive. Or it comes to the brink of "simony". Sometimes it crosses that red line.

On two occasions that come to mind, Jesus invited himself to the home of someone who was not "respectable". First, to the home of Matthew, then second, to the home of Zacchaeus. He did not promise to increase their wealth with additional blessings. Instead, here was what happened…

- In Matthew's case, he was invited to leave his lucrative career as a tax collector, in the good books of the Romans, and to join a band of disciples that focused on spiritual (not material) things and were constantly under threat from both the Romans and the Jews.

- In Zacchaeus' case, there was a sudden departure from respectability: *"[8] But Zacchaeus stood up and said to the Lord, "Look, Lord! Here and now I give half of my possessions to the poor, and if I have cheated anybody out of anything, I will pay back four times the amount."*

I wonder if any of the prophets of the prosperity gospel have signed the Giving Pledge? That is, to give half of their wealth away – to worthy causes.

Martin Luther saw the mercenary motives of the young prince – Albert of Brandenburg. He was ambitious to become the most powerful cleric in all of Germany. So even before he was old enough (by canon law) to be a bishop, and in places outside of the space where he qualified, he had already bought two bishoprics when an archbishopric came open – in Mainz. He knew that such church offices were for sale. So after some negotiation with Rome, a price was agreed. But it was more than Albert had in his treasury. So he got financing from German bankers. To pay them back, he had an "arrangement" with Pope Leo X. He could promote the sale of indulgences in any part of Germany that allowed it, and pay only fifty percent to Rome. The other fifty percent would help him to pay back his bank loans! Patronage works that way – it has to help both sides.

Prince Albert deployed a marketing whiz called Johann Tetzel (a Dominican friar) to flog indulgences throughout Germany – except in places like Saxony where it was outlawed. On theological grounds, Martin Luther just wanted to dispute this practice – internally. But his students let the cat out of the bag, and his 95 theses found their way into the public domain – thence to Tetzel, and on to Rome and the pope. All were infuriated at Luther's impertinence. That is what really got the flames of the Protestant Reformation burning hot.

The question is, where do you draw this line?

On a continent where hunger and poverty are still a fact of everyday life, how can African pastors own airplanes and mansions in London?

Paradigm Lost

When government leaders turn their positions of public service into "kleptocracy", it is called "state capture". Is there such a thing as "church capture"? This matter is closely related to good governance. Pastors who "own" their church or who operate without a proper Board in place to hold them accountable, are likely to end up in trouble.

In Matthew chapter 19, the advice of Jesus had been sought out by a rich, young ruler. He was a devoutly religious man who had done his best to observe the Law of Moses. He could not really be faulted, and God had blessed him abundantly. Here is the advice that Jesus gave him:

[21] *Jesus said to him, "If you want to be perfect, go, sell what you have and give to the poor, and you will have treasure in heaven; and come, follow Me."*

Jesus was clearly putting some distance between wealth and following him. Usually, Jesus was not so direct. His favourite teaching method was parables – which line up very well with what some call "African indirection". How can his generic teaching on wealth be squared with this latest trending among Africa church leaders?

[19] *"There was a rich man who was dressed in purple and fine linen and lived in luxury every day.* [20] *At his gate was laid a beggar named Lazarus, covered with sores* [21] *and longing to eat what fell from the rich man's table. Even the dogs came and licked his sores.*

[22] *"The time came when the beggar died and the angels carried him to Abraham's side. The rich man also died and was buried.* [23] *In Hades, where he was in torment, he looked up and saw Abraham far away, with Lazarus by his side.* [24] *So he called to him, 'Father Abraham, have pity on me and send Lazarus to dip the tip of his finger in water and cool my tongue, because I am in agony in this fire.'*

^{25} *"But Abraham replied, 'Son, remember that in your life-time you received your good things, while Lazarus received bad things, but now he is comforted here and you are in agony.* ^{26} *And besides all this, between us and you a great chasm has been set in place, so that those who want to go from here to you cannot, nor can anyone cross over from there to us.'*

^{27} *"He answered, 'Then I beg you, father, send Lazarus to my family,* ^{28} *for I have five brothers. Let him warn them, so that they will not also come to this place of torment.'*

If this book is nothing else, it is a warning to my Christian brothers: The road to hell is paved with good intentions.

8. Recommended Reading

(by date of publication)

Sarah Gertrude Millin, The Burning Man, Windmill Press, 1952

James Bentley, A Calendar of Saints, Orbis, 1986

Lawrence W Henderson, A Igreja em Angola, Alem-Mar, 1990

Willem Saayman, Christian Mission in South Africa, UNISA Press, 1991

Elizabeth Isichei, A History of Christianity in Africa, Eerdmans, 1995

Willem Saayman, A Man with A Shadow: The Life and Times of Professor ZK Matthews, UNISA Press, 1996

Barbara Kinsolver, The Poisonwood Bible, Faber & Faber, 1998

Tom Hiney, On the Missionary Trail, Atlantic Monthly Press, 2000

Pagan Kennedy, Black Livingstone, Penguin, 2002